Aviation Elite Units

No 56 Sqn
RFC/RAF

No 56 Sqn
RFC/RAF

Alex Revell

Series editor Tony Holmes

Front Cover

On 30 January 1918 – a bright winter's morning – No 56 Sqn ace Capt James McCudden took off alone at 0945 hrs. The previous day the engine of his SE 5a had been fitted with high compression pistons, and McCudden hoped that they would sufficiently increase the power of his Hispano-Suiza 8B motor to enable him to catch and engage the enemy's high-flying, Maybach-powered, Rumpler Cs. After two unsuccessful engagements involving a Hannover C over Bullecourt and five Albatros scouts south of Vendhuille, McCudden saw five more German fighters climbing for height above Anneux. Determined as ever to follow his own dictum 'to destroy as many as possible of the enemy at the least risk and casualties to one's own side', the veteran ace waited until the aircraft had reached 14,000 ft before using a 5000-ft height advantage to dive on them;

'Down I went, and very quickly got behind the leader, into whom I fired a burst at very close range. He at once went down vertically, with pieces of three-ply wood falling off his fuselage, and he was seen to strike the ground by our "Archie" gunners. I hadn't time to watch him, as I was fighting four more scouts now and had my attention fully occupied. However, I got into position behind a Pfalz, and after a short burst from the good old Vickers he went down in a spiral dive and crashed also.'

The remaining three enemy scouts, in McCudden's own words 'now evinced signs of alarm'. He fired at another Albatros, which spun away, but was then attacked by a second machine from behind. McCudden quickly reversed the positions, got onto the tail of the Albatros and opened fire, but after only a short burst both guns stopped – his Lewis gun was out of ammunition, and the belt of his Vickers had broken. McCudden now felt 'awfully brave', and realising the remaining Albatros and Pfalz were 'awfully dud', stayed to fight them, chasing the scouts south of Cambrai before heading home.

The leader of the formation, Vfw Adam Barth of *Jasta* 10, flying Albatros D V 4565/17, was killed, whilst the pilot of the Pfalz – McCudden's second victory of the day, and his 46th overall – survived the crash (*Cover artwork by Mark Postlethwaite*)

First published in Great Britain in 2009 by Osprey Publishing, Midland House, West Way, Botley, Oxford OX2 0PH, UK
443 Park Avenue South, New York, NY 10016, USA
E-mail; info@ospreypublishing.com

A CIP catalogue record for this book is available from the British Library

ISBN: 978 1 84603 428 2
E-book ISBN: 978 1 84908 104 7

Edited by Tony Holmes
Page design by Mark Holt
Cover artwork by Mark Postlethwaite
Aircraft Profiles by Harry Dempsey
Index by Alan Thatcher
Printed in China through Bookbuilders

09 10 11 12   10 9 8 7 6 5 4 3 2 1

FOR A CATALOGUE OF ALL BOOKS PUBLISHED BY OSPREY MILITARY AND AVIATION PLEASE CONTACT:

NORTH AMERICA
Osprey Direct, C/O Random House Distribution Center, 400 Hahn Road, Westminster, MD 21157
E-mail – uscustomerservice@ospreypublishing.com

ALL OTHER REGIONS
Osprey Direct, The Book Service Ltd, Distribution Centre, Colchester Road, Frating Green, Colchester, Essex, CO7 7DW, UK
E-mail – customerservice@ospreypublishing.com

www.ospreypublishing.com

CONTENTS

PROMISE FULFILLED

Sunday, 30 September 1917, dawned fine and bright. In France, at Estrée Blanche aerodrome, near the River Lys, the pilots of No 56 Sqn Royal Flying Corps (RFC) had waited with some impatience for first light. The unit's score of enemy aeroplanes destroyed had reached a total of 198, and each pilot hoped to have the distinction of claiming the 200th victory. The question of which flight should perform the first patrol of the day had led to a heated discussion at dinner the previous evening, at which each of the flight commanders had put forward their own case with some force. By the rotation of patrols, however, it was B Flight's turn to fly the first patrol, and its commander, high-scoring ace Capt James McCudden, had stuck quietly but firmly to its right to do so.

The SE 5as of B Flight took off at 0745 hrs. Enemy territory was almost totally obscured by a thick ground mist, and, consequently, until the sun began to disperse it at around 0900 hrs, there was little enemy activity. At 0915 hrs McCudden attempted to lure a formation of Albatros 'V' Strutters under a formation of Bristol F 2B Fighters from No 22 Sqn, but the wary German pilots turned east, refusing the bait. Five minutes later McCudden saw five more Albatros scouts over Houthem. He attacked one of these, driving it down to 2000 ft, but failing to gain any decisive result. B Flight returned to Estrée Blanche, disgruntled by its failure to score. During the remainder of the morning and into the early afternoon a number of pilots flew solo missions, but all without result.

A and C Flights took off at 1630 hrs, with weather conditions having by now improved considerably. Capt Geoffrey Bowman led C Flight to Ypres, at which point he was forced to turn back with a burst oil tank. The remaining members of the flight – Lts Richard Maybery and Reginald Hoidge – flew on, keen to score the 199th and 200th victories for C Flight.

At 1700 hrs Maybery and Hoidge attacked five Pfalz D III scouts over Roulers. Maybery's opponent turned under him, and as he dived at the Pfalz, Hoidge came between them, forcing Maybery to break off his pursuit. Finding himself beneath a second Pfalz, he pulled down his Lewis gun and fired half a drum of ammunition at the enemy scout. The Pfalz dived away and Maybery followed, firing short bursts. The German scout continued down and crashed west of Roulers, giving No 56 Sqn its 199th victory.

Maybery then came under attack from yet another Pfalz, so he turned west and rejoined Hoidge, who had had no luck in the fight – persistent gun stoppages had robbed him of an almost certain victory.

A short while later both pilots attacked a two-seater over the eastern end of Houthulst Forest. Again, gun jams forced Maybery and Hoidge to break off their attacks, allowing the two-seater to escape to the east. They next chased a pair of two-seaters that they had spotted over the northern end of the forest, but both aircraft dived away to the east as well. The 200th victory was proving elusive. Maybery then sighted yet another two-seater, west of Menin. He dived to attack it but after a short burst his Lewis gun stopped. He had used up the drum.

Diving under the enemy machine, Maybery frantically began changing magazines, but in his eagerness and excitement he failed to place the drum correctly and it fell off, hitting him a glancing blow on the head before bouncing over the side of the cockpit! Maybery, his head spinning – a full Lewis gun drum was no mean weight – turned for home, having no more ammunition left. His Vickers gun had been inoperative throughout the patrol.

Hoidge had had no better luck. He subsequently attacked a group of four Pfalz scouts single-handedly, but his guns continued to give trouble and he was forced to break off the action and return home, having run low on fuel.

Further south, A Flight had been in action with eight enemy scouts over Comines. Flight commander Capt Gerald Maxwell had selected his opponent carefully. A full drum of Lewis and 100 rounds of Vickers 'from very close range' sent the Albatros down out of control, nose over tail. When A Flight landed back at Estrée Blanche, they found that of C Flight only Maybery had returned. They eagerly compared notes, but it was not until all the pilots had finally landed that it was established that Maybery had scored the 199th victory and Maxwell the 200th. Maybery's victim was estimated to have crashed at 1700 hrs and Maxwell's 30 minutes later.

By the time the combat reports had been made out, with 'Grandpa' Marson, the Squadron Recording Officer, presiding, it was nearly dark. The entire unit assembled outside the sheds. At the word of command from No 56 Sqn's commanding officer, Maj Richard Blomfield, the squadron's entire stock of Very lights (flares) was fired into the evening sky – 40 red, white and green lights lit up the countryside. Dinner that night was a gala affair. The food was excellent, the squadron's band played and there was 'much speechmaking'. After a great deal of high-spirited horseplay in the ante-room, the pilots went to bed, well pleased with the successes of the day, and elated and proud of the squadron's record.

The following day a letter of congratulation was received from Gen Hugh Trenchard, General Officer Commanding (GOC) the RFC in the Field. It said, in part;

'The work of this squadron has been really wonderful, and it reflects the greatest credit on you as a Squadron Commander, the Flight Commanders, pilots and the NCOs and men, and it has no doubt helped largely towards reducing the enemy to a proper frame of mind in the air.'

The 200th victory and Trenchard's letter set the seal on No 56 Sqn's growing reputation as the most successful fighter squadron in the RFC. This achievement was the culmination of five months – apart from two weeks spent defending London – of intense and fiercely contested air fighting.

EARLY DAYS

On 9 June 1916 three 2nd class air mechanics were posted from Farnborough to Fort Grange, in Gosport, Hampshire, as a nucleus flight for No 56 Sqn. By 17 June, the number of men assigned to the unit had risen to around 20, and the squadron's first commanding officer, Maj E L Gossage, had taken command. At a noonday parade on 23 June 1916, No 56 Sqn took on its own identity from No 28 Sqn (its parent unit), and on 14 July it

No 56 Sqn CO Maj Richard Graham
Blomfield was described as being
'Tremendously energetic and keen.
He was always to be seen hurrying
here and there, giving close personal
supervision to every detail of the
squadron's work – activity and
organisation personified'

moved to London Colney, a recently established large training aerodrome in
Hertfordshire. During the remainder of the year the squadron gradually
built up to full strength.

On 6 February 1917, after four more changes of command, the CO
who was to take the squadron to France, and lay the foundations of its
traditions and greatness, took command. Maj Richard Graham Blomfield,
described by one pilot as 'the prince of organisers', was determined to
make his unit the finest in France, and he chose his pilots – especially his
three flight commanders – carefully. He also left no avenue unexplored
to ensure that the NCOs and men assigned to No 56 Sqn were also the
best available, particularly those who would service and maintain the
unit's aeroplanes.

Blomfield was also a great believer in morale, and fully realising the part
that music could play in its upkeep, he formed an excellent and highly

Capt E L Foot in an SE 5 at London
Colney in April 1917. One of the
original flight commanders, Foot
was injured in a car accident on the
evening of 6 April and was unable to
fly to France with the squadron the
following morning. This photograph
clearly shows the large canopy
so disliked by the pilots. Neither
a Lewis gun or Aldis gunsight
have been fitted to this machine

professional squadron orchestra, exchanging non-musical craftsmen for ones who were. He also saw to it that a number of orchestral musicians who were then being drafted under the First Military Service Bill were taken into the RFC and sent to his squadron. Equipment officers from other squadrons were wined and dined, and names of particularly efficient mechanics in their units were gently extracted from them to also find their way into No 56 Sqn.

Knowing their importance, Blomfield selected his three flight commanders carefully. The first two were Capts Albert Ball and Ian Henry David Henderson. Blomfield's 'capture' of Ball gave the squadron an immediate reputation, for he was then the leading ace of the RFC. Credited with 30 victories, he had been awarded the Military Cross and a Distinguished Service Order with two Bars. Sent home on extended leave in the late autumn of 1916, Ball had been pressing the authorities to allow him to return to active duty in France just as No 56 Sqn was being formed at London Colney.

Capt Henderson was also a pilot of some experience, having flown with No 19 Sqn during the battles of the Somme in 1916. The third flight commander was Capt Ernest Foot, who was known throughout the RFC as 'Feet'. A brilliant pilot, he had served with Ball in No 60 Sqn – no doubt Ball had influenced Blomfield in his choice of Foot.

However, Blomfield's careful plans seemed doomed from the outset. Firstly, Henderson broke his nose and was posted away, to be replaced by Capt Cyril Marconi Crowe, a fine pre-war pilot who had served in France with Nos 4 and 8 Sqns. The bad luck continued when Crowe fell ill with measles and was taken to hospital.

The influence of Ball is apparent in Blomfield's next choice too, as Capt Henry 'Duke' Meintjes had also flown with him in No 60 Sqn. Ball also toured the various training establishments as a talent scout looking for promising pilots. Lts Gerald Constable Maxwell, Leonard Barlow and Arthur Rhys Davids were three of his recommendations. There were no doubt others, but in the coming months these three officers alone, all of whom would become high-scoring aces, were to prove Ball's ability for picking embryonic air fighters.

Capts Albert Ball (left) and Cyril Crowe pose informally for the camera at London Colney in April 1917

Capt Albert Ball is seen here in SE 5 A4850 at London Colney on 6 April 1917. This aircraft was the only SE 5 to be extensively modified before the squadron left for France. Its large windscreen was removed and a smaller 'Avro' type substituted. A new centre section was also fitted which incorporated an internal gravity-fed petrol tank, the controls to the tailplane were altered, and the seat was removed and replaced with a wooden one, which had the effect of seating Ball lower down in the aeroplane. 'Bristol type' wheels were fitted and a small head fairing added. The Vickers gun and its Constantinescu gear were also removed, its position in the top fuselage then being decking faired over. The space that this modification saved was filled with a larger capacity petrol tank. An extra Lewis gun was also installed, firing downwards through the floor of the cockpit. Most of these modifications were later removed in France by order of HQ RFC

9

Reginald Theodore Carlos Hoidge
in SE 5 A4862 at London Colney in
April 1917. This aircraft is in standard
form, awaiting fitment of both an
Aldis gunsight and Lewis gun

Capt Henry 'Duke' Meintjes had
previously served in No 60 Sqn, with
whom he had scored four victories.
Meintjes led No 56 Sqn's advance
party to Vert Galant on 5 April 1917

Efficiency was Blomfield's watchword. Although a strict disciplinarian, he was a genial man, and despite working his pilots hard during the day he turned them loose in London – only 18 miles away – at night. 'They had to be tip-top aviators and bring down Huns. Nothing else mattered', he recalled post-war.

The squadron's first aeroplane, a BE 2c, arrived on 7 August, with more following during the month – a Curtiss, some Bristol Scouts, Sopwith two-seaters and a variety of BE types.

The squadron had been designated as the first to be equipped with a new fighter in the form of the SE 5, designed by the team of F Green, H P Folland and J Kenworthy at the Royal Aircraft Factory at Farnborough. Great things were expected of the SE 5, but when Ball ferried the first example from Farnborough to London Colney on 15 March 1917, and subsequently completed a test hop around the airfield, it proved to be a great disappointment. No 56 Sqn's engineering officer, Hubert Charles, recalled 'Everybody couldn't believe that this was the SE 5 fighter? The thing looked hopeless – a joke. It was hopelessly slow, and Ball obviously didn't want to do any aerobatics in it'.

Several faults were immediately found with the SE 5, but these were mainly associated with its production rather than the scout's basic design, and Blomfield, anxious that nothing should delay the squadron leaving for France on the specified date, ordered that only essential work was to be undertaken by Charles and his mechanics. The latter remembered, 'The aim of all our efforts was simply to get the aeroplanes to fly to France with their Lewis guns, engines and controls working, and leave the questionable operability of its Vickers gun, and associated interrupter gear, until we got there'.

On 5 April an advance party of men, led by Capt Meintjes, 2Lt Maurice Kay and the adjutant, 2Lt Thomas Marson, left for France with aeroplane spares and general stores. Their destination was a small farm in northern France – Vert Galant.

DO WELL AND FEAR NOT

Snow fell on 6 April 1917, which was also Good Friday. That evening, a farewell dinner party was held in a small hotel in the nearby village of Radlett. Capt Cecil Lewis recalled that all the pilots retired early to bed strictly sober;

'It was our ambition to do what no other squadron had previously done. Namely to arrive at our aerodrome overseas without losing a single machine by the way.'

Officers pose for a photograph at London Colney prior to leaving for France. They are, in the back row (from left to right), G J C Maxwell, W B Melville, H M T Lehmann, C R W Knight, L M Barlow and K J Knaggs. In the front row (from left to right) are R C A Lewis, J O Leach, R G Blomfield, A Ball and R T C Hoidge. This historic photograph was commissioned by the father of H N Charles, the squadron's engineering officer

No 56 Sqn SE 5s lined up on London Colney aerodrome on the morning of 7 April 1917

Kenneth John Knaggs on the morning of 7 April 1917. He is wearing the lifebelt that was issued for the flight across the Channel. It remains unclear as to whether these were actually worn for the crossing

Above right
'Revving up and ready to go'. Ball, in SE 5 A4850, is slightly ahead of the other machines

The first SE 5 (in the air on the extreme right), flown by C A Lewis, took off on 7 April at approximately 1155 hrs. Ball, in A4850, is nearest the camera

The next morning all was ready. The waiting was over. The aerodrome was the scene of organised activity, and by 1045 hrs all the pilots were in their cockpits. Ball, as usual, was bare-headed. He had met and become engaged to a local girl during his time at London Colney, but he had asked her not to come to see him leave that morning. He handed a letter to her brother. On the back, scribbled in pencil, was the message '7th April 1917. 8.30. Goodbye Bobs. Albert'.

At 1155 hrs the SE 5s were 'revving up and ready to go'. At a signal from Maj Blomfield, Cecil Lewis led the squadron out onto the field. One by one they turned into the wind, took off and circled the field once, the pilots waving. Then, quite suddenly it seemed to the watchers on the ground, they were almost out of sight, flying to the east. It was exactly noon.

A mile from the aerodrome, in the village of Shenley, there is a small circular building. Dating from the eighteenth century, it was built as a lock-up to cool off the minor miscreants of the village. On panels above its two small windows is an inscription – advice to any would-be lawbreakers, yet strangely applicable as parting counsel on that April morning in 1917. 'Do well and fear not. Be sober and vigilant'.

FRANCE

After landing at St Omer for lunch, the 13 SE 5s flew to Vert Galant aerodrome, six miles south of Doullens abreast the Doullens-to-Amiens road. The squadron shared the aerodrome with the other fighter squadrons of the 9th Wing, namely Nos 66 and 19 Sqns. The Sopwith Pups of No 66 Sqn used the field to the west of the road, whilst the SPAD VIIs of No 19 Sqn and the SE 5s of No 56 Sqn flew from the larger field on the east side of the aerodrome.

On 9 April the work of modifying the SE 5s began. Engines and guns were made more reliable through a number of smaller modifications, and the large cumbersome windscreens, which were universally unpopular with the pilots, were removed. This work was not completed until 20 April, and some idea of its importance can be seen by the fact that the squadron was unable to take part in the Battle of Arras, which had begun on 9 April.

The squadrons of the RFC were particularly hard-pressed at this time. In the late summer of 1916 the Germans had begun to re-organise their experimental *Kampfeinster Kommandos*, in which a few single-seater fighters were on strength, into true fighter squadrons, each comprised of a dozen aeroplanes. These units were entitled *Jagdstaffeln* (Hunting Echelons), and the first seven were in existence by the autumn of 1916. A total of 37 *Jagdstaffeln* had been set for the spring of 1917, and by November 1916, 25 *Jasta* had been formed, and an additional seven were at the front by the end of December.

The equipment of these early *Jagdstaffeln* was superb. By the late summer of 1916 the pendulum of technical superiority in the air war had swung once more strongly in favour of the *Luftstreitkräfte*. The DH 2s and FE 8s of the RFC, which had stemmed the Fokker scourge, were themselves now outclassed by the German Albatros, Pfalz and Halberstadt fighters of the new *Jagdstaffeln*. During late March and early April 1917, the improved version of the Albatros D II, the D III, began to appear at the front, the sesquiplane wing layout giving it the V-strut configuration which was to become so familiar to the pilots of the RFC, and earn it the colloquial name of 'V' Strutter.

The fighter aeroplanes available to the RFC at this time were the Sopwith Pup, the Nieuport 17 and 23 and the SPAD VII, plus the excellent Sopwith Triplane (used exclusively by the squadrons of the Royal Naval Air Service). Although these machines were, in the main, more manoeuvrable than the German fighters, their armament consisted of just a single Lewis or Vickers gun. The Albatros, Pfalz and Halberstadt scouts were fitted with twin Spandau guns. The British machines were also appreciably slower, which meant that German pilots could avoid, initiate or break off combat at will, placing their Allied opponents at a serious tactical disadvantage.

By the beginning of the third week of April the modifications to the squadron's SE 5s had been completed, and on 19 and 20 April a great deal of test flying was done. These changes had made a significant difference to the aircraft's capabilities, and the pilots were now keyed up for the 22nd, when the squadron would complete its first war patrol in France.

At 1018 hrs that morning, and under strict orders not to cross the frontline, Ball led five SE 5s on a defensive patrol over Aix, Neuville and St Léger. Flying at 11,000 ft between Liévin and Croiselles, Ball saw an Albatros two-seater near Adinfer. He fired a red Very light and headed for the enemy aircraft. The Albatros immediately turned and dived towards its own lines, but Ball still got to within 150 yards of the machine. He fired three drums worth of Lewis rounds at the fleeing two-seater, but his shots had no visible effect and the Albatros merely steepened its dive for the safety of its lines. Mindful of their orders, the SE 5 pilots let it go. Several hours later, B Flight, led by Capt 'Duke' Meintjes, flew along the same patrol line but saw no enemy aeroplanes. It had been a disappointing day.

On the 23rd the squadron undertook its first offensive patrol. Led by Capt Cyril Crowe, C Flight took of at 0600 hrs and patrolled from Farbus to Monchy at 8000 ft until heavy and accurate anti-aircraft fire at the junction of the River Scarpe and the Canal de la Sensée forced them up to 13,000 ft. The patrol returned at 0800 hrs, having seen no enemy aircraft.

Ball had also taken off alone at 0600 hrs in a Nieuport 23. He was still unhappy with the SE 5, much preferring the more manoeuvrable Nieuport with which he had scored his early victories. Indeed, upon his return to France with No 56 Sqn, Ball had gained the approval of Gen Hugh Trenchard, GOC of the RFC, to continue using a Nieuport for his individual patrols, whilst flying an SE 5 when patrolling with the rest of the unit. Ball flew to the Douai-Cambrai area, knowing that any enemy aeroplanes making for their aerodromes in this vicinity would have to pass by him first.

At 0645 hrs, whilst patrolling over Cambrai at 8000 ft, Ball spotted a pair of enemy two-seaters – possibly Albatros C IIIs. They were below him, so he dived underneath them in order to achieve his favourite attacking position. Ball then pulled down the Lewis gun mounted on the top wing of the Nieuport, but before he could open fire the first Albatros pilot dived to the east. Unperturbed, Ball positioned his fighter beneath the second German machine and fired half a drum of Lewis rounds into it. The Albatros went down, followed by Ball (who was still firing), and crashed by the side of the Tilloy-to-Abancourt road. Both crewmen perished. Ball had scored the first victory for No 56 Sqn.

A few minutes later Ball spotted another Albatros, just south of Arras, which was using the cloud cover to mask its approach to the town. Ball again dived and attempted to come up underneath it, but the enemy pilot was an old hand and throttled back, causing the RFC ace to overshoot. For a brief moment Ball came into the sights of the enemy pilot, and a well-aimed burst hit the Nieuport in two wing spars. He dived away, and the Albatros pilot made good his escape by diving to the east. Ball finished out his patrol time, but the Nieuport would not be ready to fly again until the afternoon of 27 April. The enemy pilot had put a burst of 15 rounds into the wing spars, resulting in both lower wings having to be replaced.

At 1045 hrs Ball again took off alone, this time flying his SE 5 A4850. He attacked an all-white Albatros two-seater over Adinfer, diving underneath it and opening fire with his Lewis gun. After only five rounds the weapon jammed, so Ball broke off the action and landed at No 60 Sqn's aerodrome at Le Hameau to rectify the faulty gun. This done, he returned to the Cambrai area.

At 1145 hrs Ball chased five single-seater Albatros scouts before finally closing with them over Selvigny. He fired 150 rounds from his Vickers gun into the nearest of the German fighters, which fell away out of control before bursting into flames. The remaining enemy pilots then attacked Ball, putting five rounds into the right spar of his SE 5, four into the wings and two into the fuselage just behind the pilot's head. Using the superior speed of his scout, Ball dived away and shook them off. Some 45 minutes later he attacked another all-white Albatros C III north of Cambrai, firing half a drum of Lewis rounds into it. The Albatros dived steeply away and made a good landing, the pilot, Vfw Ebert of *Flieger Abteilung (Fl Abt) 7*, helping out his observer, Ltn Berger, who had suffered a bad neck wound.

This ended the squadron's first day of offensive patrols. Only Ball had scored, but morale was high nevertheless.

It was now decided to extend the period of time during which the squadron could fly offensive patrols. This was achieved by reducing the number of SE 5s in a patrol to three. With a saving of two machines from each flight, it was possible to fly two additional patrols. The first patrol of three left Vert Galant at 0700 hrs on the morning of 24 April. 'Duke' Meintjes, leading Cecil Lewis and Henry Lehmann, attacked several two-seaters and enemy scouts east of Arras, but all their attacks were frustrated by continual gun jams.

The second offensive patrol of the day, led by Cyril 'Billy' Crowe, had better luck. At 1110 hrs the SE 5s attacked a pair of two-seaters between Gavrelle and Bullecourt. Crowe dived and opened fire from 50 yards, but

Cecil Arthur Lewis, seen here with 'Jock', served with No 3 Sqn during the Somme battles of 1916. After his service with No 56 Sqn, Lewis flew Camels with Nos 44 and 61 and 152 Sqns. After the war, he led an extremely varied and interesting life, being a flying instructor in China in the early 1920s, a founder member of the BBC, a producer and director for the theatre and films in the 1930s, and an Oscar winner in 1938 for his screenplay of *Pygmalion*. Lewis also found time to write one of the legendary volumes on World War 1 air fighting, *Sagittarius Rising*, based on his exploits in combat. He served in the RAF in World War 2, after which he farmed in Africa before retiring to Corfu. When he died in January 1997, Lewis was the last surviving pilot of No 56 Sqn in World War 1

his Vickers gun jammed after just a few rounds. Maurice Kay, just behind Crowe, also managed to get off a few shots before the Constantinesco (CC) gear of his Vickers gun failed as well. Kay then came under determined and heavy fire from the enemy observer, but this failed to deter him. Slipping under the tail of the enemy machine, he got in a good burst of 20 rounds from his Lewis gun. Leonard Barlow attacked the same two-seater, closing to within 20 yards and firing both guns until his CC gear failed too. Before finally turning away, Barlow fired a drum of Lewis into the enemy machine, which turned over and went down out of control, finally hitting the ground near Bellone.

Crowe and Kay then joined forces with two Nieuports and, ten minutes later, attacked five Albatros scouts that had bright red tails and fuselages. Crowe attacked the nearest, firing a good burst of Vickers into it from a range of 100 yards until the gun again jammed. Seeing Crowe turn away, Kay attacked the scout, firing only his Lewis – his Vickers was also out of action. The Albatros pilot dived away. Kay followed, but at 6000 ft he came under heavy and accurate anti-aircraft fire, so he broke off the pursuit, climbed back to 11,000 ft and rejoined Crowe. Barlow now reappeared, and the three SE 5s returned to base.

The victory over the two-seater, possibly a machine from *Fleiger Abteiling (A)* 224, was shared between the three pilots, as it was considered that all three had put in good shooting at it. Crowe had seen the Albatros scout attacked by Kay land near Douai. In view of their colour, and position, it is probable that these scouts were from *Jasta* 11.

The next patrol was led by Ball, taking off at 1300 hrs. Just south of Douai, a green Albatros scout was sighted flying at 10,000 ft. Maxwell came up under its tail and fired a whole drum of Lewis rounds into the aircraft from a range of just ten yards. The Albatros rolled over onto its back and dived towards Hamel. Maxwell and Knight followed it down to 1500 ft, at which point they were forced to clear the area after coming under heavy fire from the ground. Both Maxwell and Knight were credited with a share in the destruction of the Albatros, but Maxwell had no doubt. That night he wrote in his diary, 'Got my first Hun. Single-seater Albatros scout. Came up under his tail to about ten yards and loosed off. Enemy aircraft dived to earth and crashed'.

A young Scot who was outwardly calm but inwardly jubilant, Maxwell would claim a further 25 aeroplanes destroyed before the end of the war.

The next patrol of three SE 5s left Vert Galant at 1500 hrs, anxious to play their part in this day of success. They were not to be disappointed. Almost at the end of their patrol time, the pilots attacked five Albatros scouts – one green and four red – over Fresnoy. Kenneth Knaggs selected the green Albatros and the pilot made the fatal mistake of diving away. Knaggs gave the Albatros two bursts from his Lewis gun and it spun down over the Arras-to-Douai road, just east of Fresnes.

At dinner that night there was an air of jubilation, the pilots excited with the successes of the day. Three enemy machines had been brought down. They had met and routed the enemy fighters, and had found that the performance of the SE 5 had enabled them to initiate or break off combats at will. Ball's dislike of the aircraft seemed to be unfounded. However, there was one problem – the almost universal gun jams that had possibly robbed them of additional victories. They had to be solved.

Low clouds and bitter cold made flying impossible the following day, and the next patrol was not flown until the evening of 26 April when Ball led four SE 5s out at 1815 hrs. Soon after taking off the patrol split up, Ball flying to his favourite hunting ground west of Douai. Barlow, Lehmann and Melville saw no action, but a few miles to the southeast, the RFC ace was fighting for his life.

Arriving over the Douai area, Ball had watched a formation of FE 2ds approaching him from the direction of Cambrai on their way home. As he watched the ungainly pushers, Ball observed a number of enemy scouts taking off from an aerodrome to the east of Cambrai – possibly the base of *Jasta* 3 at Awoingt. The ace 'went and sat over Cambrai', waiting until the enemy scouts had reached 6000 ft. He then dived on the nearest fighter, closing to within 20 yards and firing a full drum of Lewis and 50 rounds of Vickers into the white-painted Albatros. For once his guns worked splendidly, and the German fighter went down out of control and crashed in a small wood northeast of Cambrai.

Ball turned for the British lines, but his retreat was cut off by the remaining five enemy scouts who had managed to get to the west of him. He made straight for them, firing his Vickers, but the enemy pilots refused to scatter, boxing Ball in and forcing him to turn continually to escape their fire. He finally managed to evade their attacks and broke free, the enemy machines in pursuit. One of the German pilots outdistanced his companions, and Ball turned to face him, firing both guns. The Albatros, flown by Vfw Eisenhuth of *Jasta* 3, burst into flames along its right side and went down. The rest of the enemy pilots now caught up with Ball, but he successfully evaded their fire, flew to the southwest and finally crossed the frontlines at dusk.

Weather conditions were again bad on 27 April, and only slightly better the next day. Two patrols took off in the morning but saw no action, reporting low cloud and poor visibility. An afternoon patrol left the ground at 1650 hrs and saw plenty of action, however. Intercepting three Albatros two-seaters over Cambrai, Ball fired a red light and went down alone through the cloud cover to within 150 yards of the enemy machines. His attack was frustrated by gun jams, and he climbed back through the clouds to rejoin his flight. Clearing his jams, Ball again descended through the clouds and renewed his attack on the two-seaters, one of which he forced down. Ball then dived on the third enemy two-seater. This time he made no mistake, and it crashed at Fontaine, just west of Cambrai.

Due to the heavy cloud cover in the area, Ball had lost contact with the other SE 5s during this engagement, so he 'sat above the clouds until a two-seater Albatros came up above them at Épéhy'. The enemy machine dived away from Ball's attack and, intent on the chase, he followed it down to within 500 ft of the ground. The German anti-aircraft gunners put up a tremendous barrage to assist their fellow countrymen, shooting Ball's controls away. The SE 5 fell into a spin, but the ace managed to regain control and fly gingerly back to Vert Galant with only his left elevator fully working, and this with only one top wire intact.

Ball taxied the damaged SE 5 to the hangars, the elevators flapping loose and the nose of the scout covered in black fluid from a riddled oil tank. He climbed shakily from the cockpit, calling angrily for a rag, his face and shoulders smothered in oil. Wiping off the oil as best he could, Ball literally stamped to the sheds. Twenty minutes later his Nieuport left the ground, a still-furious Ball at the controls. He returned at 2020 hrs, the last of the squadron's scouts to be out. Ball had seen nothing on which to vent his anger, perhaps fortunately for him, as the day of the brave, headstrong, non-tactical fighter was coming to an end. Cunning was now needed to survive following the reorganisation of the German fighter force.

Gerald Maxwell was also a victim of accurate anti-aircraft fire that same day. Whilst patrolling at 10,000 ft, his SE 5 was hit in the elevators and radiator. His engine finally seized over the trenches at Combles, east of Albert, and he force-landed at Station 126 on the Decauville railway. Maxwell later recorded in his diary, 'Complete wreck. Engine fell out of machine and machine turned right over. Me not hurt. Hit ground at about 140 mph'. Although remarkably unhurt, Maxwell was sufficiently shaken to enter the incident on the wrong day of his diary.

On the morning of 29 April weather conditions were still poor. At 0900 hrs Capt Meintjes led his flight from Vert Galant with orders to patrol between Vitry and Villers. The SE 5s were passing between the villages of Hamel and Récourt when they were attacked by six Albatros scouts, grey in colour, which came at them from 'out of the eye of the morning sun'. Meintjes, an experienced fighter pilot, immediately went into a steep climbing turn, coming out above the enemy scouts. He dived to attack the nearest Albatros, which in turn fell away, with Meintjes following, firing both guns – for once these were working well. At 6000 ft, just prior to entering a cloud bank, the Albatros turned over onto its back and went down out of control.

Canadian Reginald Hoidge was in a tight spot, however. In their first pass the enemy fighters had shot through his elevators, ailerons and back spar, one accurate burst hitting the SE 5 just behind his head. His Vickers gun control wire had broken prior to crossing the lines and his Lewis was now jammed. Keeping extraordinarily calm for an inexperienced pilot, Hoidge used the superior climb and manoeuvrability of his fighter to get above the enemy scouts. With remarkable courage he then dived at the nearest one, forcing the Albatros pilots to break off the engagement and dive away. All the SE 5s made it back to Vert Galant.

The third patrol of the day, made by Crowe, Leach and Kay, sent an Albatros two-seater down out of control over Bugnicourt, before flying to the Cambrai area. Here they were attacked by a formation of enemy scouts, silver-grey in colour, and with their black crosses on white square backgrounds. There was a sharp fight, during which Crowe drove one of the enemy scouts down to 3000 ft in a steep dive out of control over Waziers. This victory for the future ace, claimed at 1500 hrs, was confirmed by a patrol of Nieuports from No 60 Sqn. After some intense fighting the German pilots cleared to the east.

Crowe reformed the patrol and led them over Douai, home of the 'Richthofen Circus', *Jagdgeschwader* Nr 1. While Kay and Leach stayed at 5000 ft, Crowe coolly dropped down to look at the enemy aerodrome. He later reported, 'the aerodrome is northeast of Douai, north of the "S" Dorignies, and quite near the town of Douai'.

Ball led the last patrol of the day. British anti-aircraft fire pointed out an enemy two-seater to them, heading north over Adinfer. The German pilot saw the SE 5s coming and dived for the safety of his own lines. Ball caught up with the two-seater over the enemy trenches north of Lens, but his guns jammed after only two shots and the pilot made good his escape.

The fighting on 30 April resulted in No 56 Sqn suffering its first casualty. The dawn patrol had had a brief, indecisive skirmish with an enemy scout, described as 'an HA Nieuport, coloured silver with a yellow nose'. The next patrol had a tragic outcome. Crowe led Leach and Kay down to attack a formation of enemy scouts that were about to engage a formation of FE 2ds. These German aircraft were from *Jasta* 20, coloured silver with green wingtips, and in Crowe's words 'a very stubborn ding-dong fight ensued, some Hun aircraft being above and some below the SE 5s'. Crowe came under attack from one of the enemy scouts. Alternately fighting and chasing each other, they moved away from the main engagement. Crowe broke off the action to rectify a gun stoppage and the enemy pilot lost sight of him. Crowe then saw him 1500 ft below and dived, firing all the way as he closed to 20 yards. The enemy scout went straight down and crashed.

Leach and Kay were both hard pressed by the other enemy pilots, who were obviously experienced. Leach zoomed above the fight, and looking down he saw Kay fighting with two of the German scouts, one of which

Maurice Alfred Kay (top) was the squadron's first casualty, being killed on 30 April 1917. He is seen here with his close friend Keith Muspratt while at the Central Flying School in 1916

had latched onto his tail. Kay went down in a wide spiral and managed to shake off this opponent, but was then attacked by another. Leach felt sure that Kay had been badly hit, and he dived at this Albatros. However, in his eagerness to rescue Kay he overshot. Zooming away, he looked down to see Kay still spinning down, with the Albatros, flown by Ltn Friedrich Mallinckrodt, on his tail. Both Kay and the Albatros hit the ground near Viller-au-Tertre and burst into flames.

Dinner that night was a quiet affair. The brave and likable Maurice Kay was dead, and his loss was keenly felt. He was the squadon's first casualty, the first of the originals to be lost. Arthur Rhys Davids wrote home 'poor Kay just vanished. So he is over in Hunland somewhere, whether dead or alive we don't know'.

The squadron was now comfortably settled into quarters at Vert Galant, the officers living in huts at the northern end of the aerodrome, separated from the flying field by the road to Beauquesne, and the men in tents scattered amongst the various outbuildings of Vert Galant farm. The farmhouse itself, beside the Doullens-to-Amiens road, housed the squadron offices and the officers' mess, the upstairs rooms providing accommodation for Maj Blomfield and several officers.

During the first patrol on 1 May, Lt Knaggs shot down an Albatros two-seater, which AA batteries confirmed crashed near Rouex. This Albatros was from *Schutzstaffel (Schusta)* 30. The pilot, Uffz Karl Sandner, was only lightly wounded, but his observer, Adam Föller, a Bavarian from Schwetzinger, was killed. In the last patrol of the day, Ball destroyed a pair of two-seaters, one crashing near Marquion and the other by the trenches southwest of Cambrai.

The weather was fine and warm on 2 May. The first patrol left Vert Galant at 0600 hrs. A longer patrol line was now being flown, starting at Bailleul, further north than the patrols had yet been. At 0730 hrs the four SE 5s, led by Meintjes, attacked a pair of Albatros two-seaters over Vitry. The enemy aeroplanes were 3000 ft below the British scouts, and the German crews, intent on their work, made easier by the bright sunny morning, had no intimation of the attack. Meintjes sent one down in a slow spiral until it hit the ground just west of the village of Corbehem.

Ball took off in the evening, accompanied by Clarence Knight. The ace knew that the fine weather would see enemy aeroplanes out in force, and he was eager to bring his victory tally to 37 so as to 'beat the Frenchman' Guynemer. There was plenty of action in the evening sky. Between Douai and the frontlines, Ball spotted four red Albatros scouts. He dived on the nearest, but was at once jumped from the rear by four others. Turning steeply, Ball caused the first of his attackers to overshoot. Pulling down his Lewis, he put 50 rounds into the enemy scout as it flashed by, fastening onto its tail and following it down to 2000 ft. He continued firing until the fighter crashed into the rough ground between Halte and Vitry.

The squadron gave a concert that night, and all went well until 2200 hrs when the fire bell rang. Ball wrote home the following evening;

'I rushed out, and Oh, picture how pleased I was when I saw my hut, greenhouse and bathroom on fire. Well, I nearly had a double fit, but that didn't put out the fire. I had taken so much trouble in getting it nice so that when I came in at night I could have a few hours real rest.'

Ball was to survive his hut by only a few days.

The Battle of Arras officially ended on 4 May. The main battlefront was to now move north for the Battle of Messines, but No 56 Sqn and the other units of the 9th Wing were to continue to patrol the Arras front until the end of the month.

During the evening patrol on the 4th, Ball shot down an Albatros that was confirmed by British AA batteries as having crashed near Graincourt. Maxwell sent another of the enemy scouts down near Sauchy-Lestrée. With the weather continuing to be fine and warm on 5 May, the 9th Wing's HQ decided to give its hard-pressed corps squadrons a well deserved rest – only the scout-equipped units flew patrols, and even these were curtailed.

In the last patrol of the day Ball flew alone to the Lens area, where he saw two 'white-winged' Albatros scouts flying towards Carvin, one slightly behind the other. Ball attacked the nearest, firing three drums of Lewis into it. The Albatros went down out of control. The second German fighter had by now turned around to attack Ball, and the two scouts flew towards each other, nose-on, firing as they closed the distance between them. Ball could see the tracers from his Vickers going straight into the Albatros, but a burst hit the SE 5 in the engine, puncturing the oil tank and covering Ball with oil. He pulled away. Although his engine had no oil pressure, it kept its revs up. Fortunately for Ball, there were no enemy aeroplanes now in sight.

Dropping to 3000 ft, he saw the two Albatros fighters on the ground, completely wrecked and lying only 400 yards from each other. The Hispano-Suiza engine in his fighter ran for three-quarters of an hour and saw Ball safely back to Vert Galant, despite it getting very little oil, which in turn meant that it had hardly any pressure. Ball landed from this combat physically exhausted. T B Marson, the squadron's recording officer, recalled;

'Flushed in the face, his eyes brilliant, his hair blown and dishevelled, he came into the Squadron office to make his report, but for a long time he was in so overwrought a state that diction was an impossibility to him.'

There was a high wind the next day, which hampered flying until the evening. Ball, who had chosen to take his Nieuport aloft, left the speedier SE 5s and flew to Douai, where he attacked four red Albatros scouts that he spotted flying towards Cambrai. He sent one down to crash just south of Sancourt.

DEATH OF AN ACE

7 May 1917, a day that was to end so tragically, began well enough. The weather was again fine and warm, but there was a hint of thunder in the air. Storm clouds began to gather in the late afternoon, with the prospect that flying would be 'washed out' for the remainder of the day. Nevertheless, orders came from the 9th Wing for the normal offensive patrol of the Douai to Cambrai area to be flown that evening. Blomfield had been told by officers serving with AA batteries in the Arras sector that a large formation of enemy scouts, understood to be from *Jasta* 11, were in the habit of congregating in the area each evening just on their own side of the lines. Blomfield had obtained permission from the 9th Wing to attack this formation, in strength, at the earliest opportunity, and the squadron mounted an unusually large patrol of 11 SE 5s that evening.

When the SE 5s took off at 1730 hrs, weather conditions were already very bad, and deteriorating. Thick layers of cumulus cloud ranged from 2000 ft up to 10,000 ft, with gaps between them. Flying at 7000 ft, Ball, leading A Flight, comprising Maxwell and Knaggs, crossed the frontlines south of the Cambrai-to-Bapaume road. C Flight (Meintjes leading Hoidge, Lewis and Melville) climbed to 7000 ft and headed northeast towards Cambrai. Crowe, took B Flight (Leach, Rhys Davids and Chaworth-Musters) 1000 ft higher and flew towards the south of the town.

B Flight ran into a thick bank of cloud over the Bois-de-Bourlon area, which took them some time to get through. Chaworth-Musters left the formation just before entering the cloud and went off in pursuit of an unidentified aeroplane. He was later shot down by Ltn Werner Voss of *Jasta* 'Boelcke' for his 25th victory.

Crowe and Leach attacked an enemy scout over Vitry, the former suffering a gun stoppage, but Leach sent the Albatros down to crash east of the town. Rhys Davids was just about to join this action when he was attacked by another Albatros approaching from the direction of Douai. The latter machine, coloured red with a green band around the fuselage, was flown by Ltn Kurt Wolff of *Jasta* 11, and his fire hit the SE 5 in the engine, undercarriage and wings – hits which Rhys Davids distinctly felt. He later wrote;

'I had heard one bullet go into my undercarriage with the deuce of a whonk, and one or two others were making themselves unpleasant by spoiling the appearance of my immaculate planes. The tiresome young man in the red bus was finally unkind enough to plonk one into my engine, which we found afterwards had made a hole six inches square in the water jacket.'

Luckily for Rhys Davids, Wolff then broke off the action and dived away. The future ace's engine finally seized, and he force-landed in a field near Herliére.

After shooting down the first Albatros, Leach was attacked by another and hit in the leg. He fainted with the pain of his wound and the SE 5 went into a spin, but petrol from his ruptured tank blew back into his face, revived him in time and he landed the damaged scout among the trenches on Vimy Ridge. Troops, fellow Canadians, lifted Leach from his cockpit and he was taken to No 4 Canadian Hospital. His leg was later amputated.

After shooting down a white 'Nieuport' type fighter, C Flight was attacked by four red Albatros scouts. Meintjes evaded his persistent attacker through an evasive spin. On regaining his height, he shot down one of the enemy scouts, which hit the ground just east of Gouy-sous-Bellone, injuring the pilot, Ltn Wolfgang von Pluschow of *Jasta* 11. Meintjes then flew to Lens and attacked another Albatros. The enemy pilot saw him coming, evaded the attack by a steep climbing turn, completely outmanoeuvred Meintjes and shot him through the wrist, blowing off the top of his control column. Meintjes managed to land near Sains-en-Gohelle and was taken to a casualty clearing station.

The squadron's pilots were now fighting various actions in the evening sky. Crowe, flying alone, had his goggles shot off by a determined enemy pilot, but he turned hard and managed to evade his attacker. He was then set upon by another formation of red Albatros scouts, but he turned west and outdistanced them. A little later, over Fresnoy, he met Ball, who was flying towards Lens.

John Owen Leach was shot down during the evening of 7 May. Although gravely wounded in the leg, he managed to land his badly damaged SE 5. Leach had to have his leg amputated

The events of the evening were now moving towards their tragic climax. Visibility was extremely bad, and Ball fired two red lights. Crowe could s ee no other aeroplanes, friendly or hostile, but continued to follow Ball, who suddenly dived on a red Albatros, firing a burst into it before overshooting. Crowe followed and also attacked the Albatros, which was almost certainly flown by Lothar von Richthofen, Manfred's younger brother. As Crowe turned for another pass, he saw Ball and the Albatros, still fighting, fly into a thick cloud. Crowe, knowing that his fuel was now very low, turned west, finally landing with the last dregs of his petrol at 'Naval 8' Squadron's aerodrome at Auchel. The time was 2015 hrs. He was the last pilot from No 56 Sqn to see Ball alive.

The RFC ace was next seen by a Ltn Franz Hailer (an officer serving with a *Flieger Abteilung*), his brother Carl and two other officers. They spotted Ball's SE 5 emerge from the low cloud at approximately 200 ft, inverted, with its propeller stopped and trailing a plume of black smoke, to crash a mile from the small village of Annoeullin. When Hailer and his companions arrived at the scene of the crash, they found that Ball had already been removed from the wrecked fuselage by a young French girl. Hailer and two other officers examined the wreckage of the SE 5. 'We all came to the conclusion that the aircraft had not been shot down in an air fight or by aircraft or anti-aircraft fire, as the dead pilot had no marks or scratches, and had not been wounded'.

A doctor who later examined Ball's body found he had a broken back and leg, fractures of the left leg and foot, a broken arm and a crushed chest.

Back at Vert Galant, anxiety turned to shocked disbelief as only five SE 5s returned of the eleven that had set out. Rhys Davids was known to be down safely, but all three flight commanders had not returned, plus Chaworth-Musters and Leach. Leonard Baker, an engine mechanic in A Flight, remembered the evening as being 'awful, just awful'. News came later that Crowe was at 'Naval 8', and that Leach and Meintjes were both in hospital, but there was still no word of Chaworth-Musters or Ball. The Mess was very quiet that night. The squadron had suffered a severe blow.

Albert Ball in SE 5 A8097. This aircraft was from the second production batch with the modified wing plan, and it was delivered to No 56 Sqn on 7 May 1917

The Germans erected this cross to mark Capt Albert Ball's grave in Annoeullin in 1917

Gerald Joseph Constable Maxwell took temporary command of A Flight after Albert Ball's death

Next morning, low clouds and lashing rain made flying impossible, the weather matching the general mood of depression in the squadron. In the afternoon, Crowe returned from 'Naval 8' and told of his last sight of Ball, whilst Blomfield visited Meintjes in hospital. Gerald Maxwell wrote home, 'We had the most awful scrap yesterday and Ball and another man are missing'. After giving news of the other casualties, he continued, 'It is absolutely awful about Ball. He is the bravest and best man in the whole British army, and it is a terrific thing for the Germans getting him, as it will buck up the whole German Flying Corps'. The day dragged to a close.

The following morning, 9 May, dawned fine and warm, but the squadron was too disorganised, both in pilots and machines, to fly any patrols. Cecil Lewis had the unhappy task of returning Ball's Nieuport to the depot at Candas. In the evening a concert was arranged – anything to raise the squadron's morale. Officers and men gathered in a large barn and the band played all the old favourites. The men sang, a corporal gave an impression of a well-know comedian, Lewis sang Stevenson's Requiem. This last was for Ball. All knew and understood. Lewis later recalled, 'The band struck up Tipperary and soon had them shouting again'.

The squadron had shown a lack of tactics on the disastrous evening of 7 May. In a sky swarming with enemy fighters the SE 5s had become separated. Even experienced pilots had been hard-pressed, but those less so had acquitted themselves well. Arthur Rhys Davids, in his first close combat, had put up a creditable show against the vastly more experienced Wolff, who already had 29 victories to his name. Writing home to his sister, telling her of the fight, Rhys Davids concluded, 'Anyway, I'm jolly lucky to have got off so light. The man up against me was obviously a far better pilot and fighter than I was – one of the few Hun pros I expect'.

On 11 May, Meintjes' replacement in the form of Capt Geoffrey Hilton Bowman arrived to take command of C Flight. The latter remembered well the mood of the squadron when he arrived. Feelings regarding the events of 7 May had hardened. Despite evidence to the contrary, there was a tendency to blame the SE 5, and Ball's dislike of the type was recalled. 'Billy' Crowe, the tall mercurial leader of B Flight, stoutly defended the SE 5 and its potential as a fighter, however. Both Bowman and Phillip Prothero (the latter not to arrive until 14 May as Ball's replacement) were six months out of date in the fast-developing art of aerial fighting, and for a while, Crowe, the only remaining experienced flight commander, ran all three flights single-handed. Indeed, he was largely responsible for restoring the squadron's morale after the heavy blow it had suffered.

On the morning of 11 May a patrol saw four red Albatros scouts attacking a two-seater. Maxwell and Lewis engaged one of the fighters, closing to within 30 yards. The enemy scout fell away out of control, and Maxwell followed it down to 7000 ft, whereupon it turned over onto its back. The fighter's fate was witnessed by British AA batteries.

The squadron suffered its fourth fatal casualty on 12 May when Augustus Jessop's SE 5 received a direct hit from *Kraftwagenflakbatterie* (*Flakbattr*) 101 *U Flazug* 159 and went down in a spin before breaking up.

Capt Bowman led his first squadron patrol on 20 May, and although there were no decisive combats fought during the flight, upon the unit's return to Vert Galand it was found that Lt Cecil French was missing. He had been claimed by Hptm Holzer of *Flakbattr* 527, having become

the second pilot from No 56 Sqn to fall victim to German flak in the space of just eight days. French was unwounded, however, and he managed to set fire to his machine before being taken prisoner.

Several patrols were flown on the 20th, and although all the flights saw plenty of action, none of them proved to be decisive until the third patrol of the day, when Capt Edric Broadberry shot down an Albatros scout out of control over Guesnain. The next victories came on 23 May, when Cecil Lewis sent an Albatros two-seater down out of control over Beaumont, and in the final patrol of the day Crowe destroyed another two-seater over Tilloy.

Crowe led the first patrol on 24 May. At 10,000 ft, south of Douai, the flight attacked a number of enemy scouts. A 'very sharp engagement' followed in which all the SE 5s fought enemy machines down to 6000 ft. One Albatros, flown by Ltn Ernst Bauer of *Jasta* 3, went down in a slow spiral, which developed into a spin and then a dive. Bauer was killed. The flight next spotted a two-seater, escorted by five Albatros D IIIs that were some 2000 ft above it. Whilst the remainder of the flight stayed above to prevent any interference by the escorting Albatros scouts, Hoidge and Rhys Davids dived to attack the two-seater, shooting it down in flames

Cyril Marconi 'Billy' Crowe was the original commander of B Flight, and his example and teaching did much to raise morale after the casualties of 7 May 1917. Crowe would serve two tours of duty with No 56 Sqn

over Gouy-sous-Bellone. The enemy fighters made no attempt to protect their charge, sheering off instead as the SE 5s climbed up to their height.

Reforming, the flight then caught another two-seater over Sans. Rhys Davids wounded the observer and the enemy machine went down, smoking badly.

Crowe and B Flight were again in action the next morning, the former being attacked by an Albatros D III that had a 'very yellow fuselage'. The enemy pilot overshot in his attack and attempted to zoom back up to a higher altitude. Crowe, finding himself directly under the Albatros, pulled down his Lewis gun and fired an entire drum at point blank range into the belly of the enemy scout. The fighter rolled over onto its back and went down between Dourges and Courcelles.

Rhys Davids and Keith Muspratt had also been successful. The latter pilot had actually taught Rhys Davids to fly back in England, and pupil and teacher attacked a two-seater, Muspratt from the side and Rhys Davids from underneath. The enemy machine, pouring smoke, went down to crash by the side of the Lens-to-Douai road. Uffz Wihelm Miltner and Vfw Ferdinand Wens of *Schutzstaffel* 24b, in Albatros C VII No C.1237/16, were both killed.

On 26 May, 2Lt Jack Toogood failed to return from patrol. He was seen attacking a pair of two-seaters, and the German credited his demise to Vfws Dietz and Woidt of *Schutzstaffel* 19. However, Toogood later wrote from captivity to say that he had been hit by a piece of anti-aircraft shell, which had almost severed his right leg. Having landed behind German lines and been taken prisoner, his leg was later amputated.

On 27 May, Leonard Barlow attacked a two-seater over Plouvain, killing the observer and riddling the enemy machine. The enemy pilot dived steeply then flattened out. Barlow resumed his attack, and at 3000 ft he shot off the two-seater's port wings. It spun down 'like an arrow', and after falling for another thousand feet its starboard wings also broke off. The aircraft crashed just north of Pouvain and burst into flames, killing Uffz Max Hofmeier and Ltn Adam Wolff of *Fl Abt (A)* 288.

Barlow then attacked another two-seater, sending it down to crash within a mile of the first. After an indecisive fight with one of the two-seaters, Rhys Davids fought with an Albatros scout, hitting it in the engine and forcing it to land. He later attacked another two-seater, which began to glide down, its engine stopped. Rhys Davids found himself at low altitude at the successful conclusion to this engagement, and whilst flying back to British lines, his SE 5 was hit in the petrol tank and radiator by ground fire. He force-landed east of Bully-Grenay, turning the scout over in a shell hole. Rhys Davids emerged from the wreckage unhurt.

In the general fighting, Crowe had attacked an Albatros scout, which crashed in a field near Erchin. 2Lt Edgar Lloyd failed to return, however, having been shot down by Ltn Altmaier of *Jasta* 33 and taken prisoner. In an evening patrol, Prothero shot an Albatros down out of control, as did Broadberry and Lewis. Capt Bowman also despatched a two-seater in a slow spin over Auberchicourt.

The next morning, B Flight saw a great deal of action. Seven hostile scouts were seen, but as the SE 5 pilots flew towards them they were joined by an additional six machines. This enemy formation made no move to attack the British fighters, and Hoidge and Melville went down to attack a pair of two-seaters instead. Suddenly, a Nieuport from No 60 Sqn, flown by unit CO (and future ace) Maj A J L Scott, dived straight in among the enemy scouts, firing a good burst at close range, before zooming up to join the SE 5s. As though this were a signal, the No 56 Sqn aircraft and the Nieuport then dived to attack the enemy scouts, and a general engagement began.

Barlow forced one Albatros to land and Muspratt got to within ten yards of another and sent it down out of control. Hoidge and Melville, busy with the two-seaters, were attacked by several of the enemy scouts. Hoidge carried on after the two-seaters, but Melville turned to meet the threat and saw Maj Scott shoot down another enemy machine. Despite the fierceness of the fighting, only one of the squadron's pilots had scored – Muspratt was credited with a scout out of control.

Later the same morning, Prothero, Broadberry and Wilkinson escorted the Martinsydes of No 27 Sqn that were sent to bomb the railway station at Busigny. On the way home Prothero saw 15 Albatros scouts, but only one of them was actually making an attack on the bombers. Prothero dived on the scout and shot it down. During this escort Geoffrey Wilkinson was wounded by anti-aircraft fire, but he managed to bring his badly damaged SE 5 back to Vert Galant. His wound was 'slight', but he was taken to hospital nevertheless.

Keith Knox Muspratt learned to fly at 16 while still attending Sherborne School. On joining the RFC, he became an instructor. After scoring eight victories with No 56 Sqn, Muspratt was posted to Martlesham Heath as a test pilot, where he was subsequently killed in a flying accident on 19 March 1918

ESTREE BLANCHE

Low cloud and mist curtailed war flying for the next two days. On 31 May, the 9th Wing headed north for the coming Battle of Messines, and its fighter units (Nos 19, 66 and 56 Sqns) moved to the large aerodrome that was officially named Liettres, but which was better known throughout the RFC as Estrée Blanche.

With its departure from Vert Galant, the squadron had completed its first seven weeks in France. In 35 days of fighting it had claimed 23 enemy aeroplanes destroyed, and another 34 sent down out of control, for the loss of ten pilots. No 56 Sqn had weathered the crippling losses of 7 May – crippling both in terms of quantity and quality – and was about to enter perhaps its most successful period. Indeed, the unit's exploits over coming months would see its fame spread throughout the RFC and even to 'the other side of the hill' to the messes of the German air force.

On 4 June a morning patrol by B Flight saw a great deal of action. Rhys Davids was flying alone until he joined up with some Sopwith Pups from No 46 Sqn. Seeing a strong force of enemy scouts being attacked by Sopwith Triplanes from 'Naval 1' Squadron and three Nieuport 17s from No 1 Sqn, Rhys Davids and the Pups joined in the mêlée. The fighting gradually broke up into smaller combats, Rhys Davids noting 'All five Hun aircraft, especially the leader (red fuselage, red, grey and black wings, V-strut type struts, pilot wearing a grey fur flying hat) manoeuvred very well'. These Albatros were from *Jasta* 28, and the pilot described by Rhys Davids was probably Ltn Karl Schafer, the scouts' *Staffelführer*.

During the general fighting, Rhys Davids saw an Albatros going down, its propeller stationary, and Thomas Dickinson spiralling down with two

Thomas Malcolm Dickinson was wounded in action and taken prisoner on 4 June 1917

Dickinson's SE 5 A8920 'B4' is seen here in German hands

enemy scouts on his tail. Although Rhys Davids made no claim, he was credited with an Albatros scout from this action. However, from a combat report by Fullard of No 1 Sqn, it seems more likely that the Albatros scout was shot down by Dickinson *before* he was himself brought down by Vfw Wittekind of *Jasta* 28. A note was later dropped by the Germans, signed by Dickinson – 'I have been wounded in both legs and am being well looked after'.

On 5 June came notification of awards of the Military Cross (MC) to Capt Crowe, Rhys Davids, and Hoidge.

There was a great deal of aerial activity the following day as the commencement of the Battle of Messines drew near. During a morning patrol Bowman shot down an Albatros scout, the pilot of the latter machine being unaware of the SE 5's presence until 50 rounds smashed into his machine. Seeing Hoidge hard pressed by three other enemy scouts, Bowman went to his aid and sent one down out of control. There were several more German fighters above them, and the patrol re-crossed the frontlines at 4000 ft. Once back at Estrée Blanche, Bowman commented that the whole experience had been 'Very unpleasant'. Harold Hamer was killed during the patrol when he fell victim to future ace Vfw Rudolf Francke of *Jasta* 8 for his second victory.

Leonard Monteagle Barlow enjoyed a highly successful tour with No 56 Sqn, scoring 20 victories. Barlow was killed in a flying accident in England on 5 February 1918 while testing a Sopwith Dolphin at Martlesham Heath

The Battle of Messines opened on 7 June. Zero hour was at 0310 hrs, and ten minutes later Leonard Barlow took off alone. His duty was to strafe the German aerodromes at Bisseghem and Reckem, and Barlow was at a height of just 400 ft when he located the former. Bisseghem was situated right alongside a mineral water factory – a fact which Barlow ascertained by reading the advertisements on the factory wall! Barlow flew twice along the length of the hangars, firing both guns, then went down to 20 ft and gave the hangars another burst.

Barlow then spotted a goods train, and he attacked this from 50 ft. The locomotive stopped in a cloud of steam and smoke, Barlow having twice flown along its length, firing all the time. Tiring of this, he then flew to Wevelgem and strafed some troops in the main street, scattering them into the roadside houses. After attacking the railway junction, Barlow flew at 50 ft along the Menin road to Reckem aerodrome. As at Bisseghem, there was no sign of any activity, but as he fired on the sheds a solitary machine gun opened up. Barlow silenced it. With all his Lewis gun ammunition now expended, Barlow made for home. A two-seater over Reckem fired a burst at the SE 5 as Barlow passed under it, shooting away his left elevator, but he landed safely at 0500 hrs. This action earned Barlow an MC.

While Barlow was out, the first squadron patrol saw a great deal of action. Rhys Davids sent down an enemy scout, possibly Fritz Kühn of *Marine-Feld Jasta* 1 who crashed near Staden and later died of his wounds, and Harry Rogerson claimed another. The next patrol spotted a pair of two-seaters over Poelcappelle. Broadberry attacked one, and later recalled that 'the enemy machine flopped about and went down out of control'. He then chased another two-seater for two-and-half miles before shooting it down to crash in a field near Ledeghem.

All these patrols strafed ground targets, and after firing at transport on the Hollebeke-to-Houthem road, Lewis attacked two Albatros which were fighting an RE 8. Driving off one, Lewis sent the other down to crash 'straight into Wervicq'. This was possibly the machine flown by Ltn Ernst Wiessner of *Jasta* 8.

The day had gone well. On the ground, the British troops had achieved all their objectives. The squadron had strafed enemy troops, brought down five enemy aeroplanes and Barlow's morning aerodrome attack on Bisseghem had inflicted significant damage on the enemy. Morale was high in No 56 Sqn.

The pace on 8 June was more leisurely. Hoidge shot down a pair of two-seaters during the day and Muspratt flew the first operational flight to be made in a 200 hp SE 5a (A8923). Weather conditions curtailed war flying

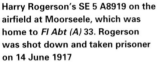

Harry Rogerson's SE 5 A8919 on the airfield at Moorseele, which was home to *Fl Abt (A)* 33. Rogerson was shot down and taken prisoner on 14 June 1917

for the next few days. Only one patrol was flown on 12 June, Bowman forcing an enemy scout to land on the aerodrome at Reckem.

The weather was better on the morning of 14 June. In an afternoon patrol, Bowman first destroyed a two-seater, which was confirmed by AA batteries. He then sent an enemy scout down out of control tail first, the aircraft eventually falling in a series of side slips until it hit the ground. Bowman wrote in his logbook, 'Shot down enemy scout which nearly fell on Maj Sanday. Confirmed by him'. Lewis had shot another enemy scout off Bowman's tail during the course of this engagement, and he watched it land on the enemy aerodrome at Lendelede. Harry Rogerson had been shot down by Ltn Küppers of *Jasta* 6, however, the British pilot being taken prisoner.

Maxwell and Prothero shot down a two-seater on 15 June, the enemy machine crashing near Fort Carnot. Crowe destroyed another the next day, which crashed near Passchendaele. Kenneth Knaggs was wounded during this patrol, the pilot being taken to hospital and struck off squadron strength. The second patrol was badly hit by 'Archie' – the RFC's nickname for anti-aircraft fire. Broadberry had all his aileron controls shot away, and only his superb piloting skills enabled him to return, earning him the cryptic comment in the squadron record book 'Hit by hostile anti-aircraft fire and obliged to return'.

On 17 June, Harry Spearpoint and William Turner-Coles were both shot down and taken prisoner. The former had fallen victim to Ltn Krebs of *Jasta* 6, while Turner-Coles was downed by both Ltn Pollandt of *Jasta* 6 and the crew of a two-seater that he had been attacking – Uffz Heidingsfelder

This photograph of William Turner-Coles was taken in 1916 for his Royal Aero Club Certificate No 2805. Turner-Coles was shot down and taken prisoner on 17 June 1917

Turner-Coles' crashed SE 5 A8922, showing how fortunate he was to escape being shot down uninjured

Above
Harry Spearpoint's SE 5 A4862,
marked 'C3', down behind German
lines on 17 June 1917

Right
Spearpoint's utter dejection after his
capture is only too evident in this
photograph. The German officer
facing the camera is Ltn Hailer

and Ltn Romberg of *Fl Abt (A)* 292, who were awarded the victory. Turner-Coles was helped from the wreckage of his machine by a Ltn Fuerholzer, who took him to a dugout and gave him a strong coffee. Seventeen years later they were to meet again, in Shanghai. Lewis avenged Spearpoint by shooting down Pollandt, who was wounded.

ENGLAND – A BRIEF INTERLUDE

On 13 June a large formation of Gotha bombers had targeted London for the first time. Included in the 594 people killed or injured were 43 dead children. A public outcry for a more efficient defence against the Gothas bought No 56 Sqn back from France on 21 June, B and C Flights being stationed at Bekesbourne, in Kent, and A Flight at Rochford, in Essex. The rest was welcome after the gruelling offensive patrols. Family members arrived and a social atmosphere developed, with dinners, dances, flying displays and concerts. One visitor to Bekesbourne was Capt James McCudden, who noted the squadron's 'wonderful spirit'. Blomfield, who

was impressed with the young pilot's keenness, determined that McCudden should come to No 56 Sqn for his next tour of duty in the frontline.

The Gothas failed to reappear, so the squadron flew back to France on 5 July, arriving back at Estrée Blanche at 5.00pm. The next day the Gothas again bombed London.

Back in France, morale was high in No 56 Sqn, the pilots being both refreshed and keen to get back into action. The first patrol on 7 July saw a great deal of fighting, with no positive result, but enemy 'Archie' was again troublesome. Hoidge had his pressure pipe and exhaust hit and Rhys Davids' propeller was shot through and wing spars shattered. Flying an SE 5a at the time, he reported 'In pursuing the Albatros scouts, the 200 hp SE 5a gave me a little extra climb and speed, which was most useful'.

Far left
'Billy' Crowe's comfortable pose against the nose of an SE 5 at Bekesbourne typifies the relaxed attitude to both life and war of the B Flight commander

Left
Thomas 'Grandpa' Marson, the squadron recording officer, and Crowe, still in slippers and pyjamas, fool around at Bekesbourne

Picnic lunch party at Bekesbourne on 5 July 1917. Arthur Rhys Davids, left, and Richard Maybery relax with Maybery's mother (2nd right) and Maybery's cousins, Nasra and Ruth Eadon. Before the squadron returned to France, Nasra (left) and Arthur Rhys Davids had come to an 'understanding'. Note the improvised table – an aeroplane wheel on two boxes

Bowman's flight claimed three enemy scouts in a later patrol, but Lewis had been wounded. 'I felt a white hot rod flipped along the round of my back'. Blomfield thought Lewis' wound – a long red furrow had been seared across his back – 'delightful'. 'Hello. You've got a cushy one. Splendid. You'll be able to put up a wound stripe now'. Lewis was sent home six days later.

The weather on 10 July was bad so the pilots decided to pass the time by painting their SE 5s in a variety of colour schemes in emulation of the German pilots that they had been meeting. Broadberry's engine mechanic, Len Baker, painted a fearsome dragon on the nose and fuselage of his SE 5, while another machine carried a painting of a Spanish dancer and the name

Arthur Rhys Davids and Thais, the daughter of 'Grandpa' Marson, at Bekesbourne. Thais was described as being 'a delightful girl aged eight who has stepped straight out of a Greek vase – a great mop of gold hair and eyes of watery blue'

C A Lewis, G H Bowman,
I Henderson, V Cronyn, A Rhys
Davids and Thias Marson at
Bekesbourne. This photograph
perfectly captures the informality
of life on a wartime aerodrome in
England in 1917

Conchita. A third SE 5 was 'striped red and white, and looked like a zebra'.
Maxwell's scout had a bright red nose. However, the 9th Wing learnt of this
'frivolity' and ordered the schemes to be removed.

On 11 July, Phillip Prothero shot down an Albatros that turned over on its
back and went down, 'turning over and over'. Broadberry put a two-seater in
a spin and Eric Turnbull sent another down in a series of sideslips.

The next day saw heavy and intense fighting, with a pair of two-seaters
attacked over Roulers. Barlow's fire stopped the engine of one, which glided
down. Rhys Davids saw five enemy machines that were 'new type scouts –
climb not very remarkable but speed fairly good. Very small black crosses
with a square-ended top plane'. Rhys Davids sent one of these down out of

Arthur Rhys Davids in SE 5 A4563
at Bekesbourne. The flight marking
'B6' has been applied forward of
the cockade

control over Roncq, then attacked a DFW from *Fl Abt* 7, crewed by Ltn Eugen Mann and Uffz Albert Hahnel. The DFW dived steeply from 7000 ft, followed by Rhys Davids, who came under attack from an Albatros. Rhys Davids was unaware of this danger, but Ian Henderson shot the Albatros down over Zanvoorde. The DFW was now down to 1500 ft, but Rhys Davids was forced to leave it when his engine began to cut out. The enemy aircraft attempted to turn east on three separate occasions, but was prevented from doing so by Keith Muspratt. Hahnel tried to put the DFW down near Armentières, but it bounced, crashed into a pond and Hahnel and both crewmen were taken prisoner.

The second patrol of the day, performed by A Flight, suffered two casualties. At 14,000 ft over Menin, it was jumped by 15 Albatros from various *Jasta*. Edric Broadberry, John Turnbull and Ernest Messervy were all shot down in the first attack. Broadberry, flying at the rear of the formation, was the first hit. 'The instrument panel was hit, there was a sharp burning pain in the calf of my right leg and the engine began to splutter, then it petered right out'. Broadberry put the SE 5 into a spin and pulled out at 2000 ft.

'I realised that I was about ten or twelve miles over the enemy side of the lines and I did not have enough height to glide to our side. I quickly switched over to the gravity fuel tank, which was housed in the centre section of the top plane, and switched on the ignition again. To my great relief the engine picked up and I was able to cross the lines to our side and land at Bailleul aerodrome'. Broadberry went into the Mess, where his leg 'started to hurt'. Taking off his flying boot, he found it 'full of blood'. The pilot was taken to a casualty clearing station.

Turnbull, shot through both legs, force-landed at Le Becque and was also taken to a casualty clearing station. Messervy had been hit in the engine and force-landed at Poperinghe.

DFW C V 799/17, crewed by Ltn Eugen Mann and Uffz Albert Hahnel, was shot down by Rhys Davids and Muspratt on 12 July 1917. Captured aeroplanes were given a G Number, in this case G 53. The DFW was one of the most successful German two-seaters. Introduced in the closing months of 1916, it equipped the *Flieger Abteilung* of the *Luftstreitkräfte* until the early months of 1918. Although James McCudden shot down at least nine of the type while with No 56 Sqn, the DFW, when flown by an experienced crew, was no easy opponent, as witness McCudden's combat with one on 12 December 1917

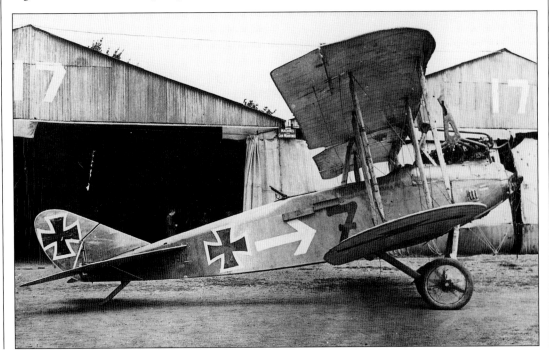

Broadberry was a great loss to the squadron. With the sole exception of Hoidge, he was scoring quicker and more often than any other member of the unit. Len Baker recalled the events of the day;

'Then came a bad, sad day. He (Broadberry) was shot down and I went after him. A thorough gentleman. To see "Mr B" coming in to land, or rather just before, was something one never saw on another SE. A steep dive, engine on full bore and only just skimming the ground before pulling out. I spoke to him about it. "Oh", he said. "She'll come out all right. I'm not going to get killed in this war". But he felt rather sad when he shot another down. He was very tenderhearted. I was sorry to lose him.'

Broadberry was the 16th victim of Oblt Eduard Dostler, the *Staffelführer* of *Jasta* 6.

The last patrol of 12 July day saw No 56 Sqn engage enemy aviators who were described by Bowman as 'some remarkably good pilots and some remarkably bad pilots'. Bowman forced one scout down. Another, painted yellow, turned over onto its back after being attacked by Hoidge. David Wilkinson sent another down 'smoking'. This fight, involving C Flight, was one of the largest of the day, with some 60 aeroplanes being engaged. The 12th had seen No 56 Sqn involved in the heaviest air fighting it had experienced to date. German formations were becoming larger, and these, attracting smaller formations of British scouts, sparked off large-scale combats.

In the last patrol of 13 July, B Flight did a great deal of fighting. Barlow shot an Albatros down out of control over Moorslede, smoke pouring from its engine, before tackling another that turned over onto its back and went down in a flat spin. That same day Cecil Lewis left the unit and Crowe was hospitalised. Maxwell, thinking of the original pilots who had flown out to France in April, commented in his diary. 'Only four left in Squadron now – Barlow, Hoidge, Rhys Davids and myself'.

Edric William Broadberry scored eight victories in just under a month. Until he was wounded on 12 July 1917, Broadberry, with the sole exception of 'Georgie' Hoidge, was scoring quicker than any other pilot of the squadron

Gerald Joseph Constable Maxwell in the cockpit of his SE 5a in the summer of 1917. The sides of the cockpit have been bulged to give the pilot more elbow room

The German Albatros fighter was the mainstay of the *Jagdstaffeln* until the introduction of the Fokker D VII in the spring of 1918, and there were large numbers still in service at the Armistice. Shown here is an Albatros D V, which was a development of the Albatros D III

On 16 July Bowman shot down Vfw Fritz Krebs of *Jasta* 6. The Albatros went down with its engine full on to crash at the eastern end of the peacetime racecourse in Polygon Wood. Maybery hit the pilot of another Albatros, who slumped forward in his seat and his machine went down in a vertical dive. Robert Jardine claimed yet another of the enemy scouts, which flew straight into the ground. Jardine's engine, having been hit by enemy fire, duly seized up, forcing him to land in a field. The SE 5 overturned and its fuselage broke in half, but Jardine emerged from the wreckage unhurt. He was claimed as a victory by Ltn Hermann Göring (his ninth of 22), *Staffelführer* of *Jasta* 27.

The following day saw another large fight – SE 5s, Sopwith Camels, FE 2ds, DH 5s and Sopwith Triplanes all fighting between 25 to 30 enemy machines. No 56 Sqn was credited with only one victory, shared between the pilots of B Flight.

On 20 July, C Flight forced an Albatros to land behind the enemy trenches northeast of Wieltje, but on returning it was found that Lts Jardine and Messervy were missing. They had both been shot down and killed.

The next evening, James McCudden, on a refresher course with No 66 Sqn, flew a patrol with A Flight. There was again a great deal of fighting in the evening sky, and McCudden helped to 'put the draught up some V Strutters' by shooting at a silver-grey Albatros, which 'turned east and wobbled laterally'. McCudden later made no claim from the evening's fighting, considering that the Albatros was under control, but Rhys Davids was credited with a black and white Albatros and Prothero was credited with another, which went down out of control over Langemarke. Canadian Verschoyle Cronyn was credited with a large green and white two-seater for the squadron's 100th victory.

The fighting continued with the same intensity over the next few days, but no further victories were scored until Hoidge claimed an Albatros out of control on 23 July and Richard Maybery forced one scout to land and its companion to crash.

The largest dogfight of the war to date took place on the evening of 26 July. Enemy two-seaters were working at 5000 ft, and 3000 ft above them Albatros scouts were fighting with the DH 5s of No 32 Sqn as the latter tried to attack the two-seaters. Between 12,000 ft and 14,000 ft, ten Albatros were fighting the SE 5s of No 56 Sqn, the Camels of No 70 Sqn and the SPAD VIIs of No 19 Sqn. At 17,000 ft, more Albatros were fighting with the Sopwith Triplanes of the Naval squadrons.

During the course of this large-scale action, Barlow sent an Albatros down out of control and Maxwell destroyed a two-seater. To negate these successes, Phillip Prothero was shot down and killed by Vfw Muth of *Jasta* 27, his SE 5 going down in pieces after its starboard wings broke off.

The next day a formation of eight FE 2ds from No 20 Sqn was used as 'bait' to lure enemy scouts over Polygon Wood, where British fighters from the 9th Wing and Sopwith Triplanes of the Naval squadrons would be waiting. The trap succeeded, with 20 enemy scouts attacking the FE 2ds. Hoidge shot down a black and white striped Albatros northeast of Roulers, while Bowman, who had only one gun working, was attacked by two enemy scouts and driven down to 4000 ft. He was saved by Maybery, who shot an enemy fighter off his tail. Bowman turned for the lines, but was attacked by another Albatros – 'this machine seemed to be red all over, and was very well flown'.

With one gun still out of action, Bowman was forced down to 1000 ft, flying straight into the eye of the setting sun. Although he finally outmanoeuvred the enemy pilot and shot him down west of Roulers, he was still not out of trouble, for he was attacked by another Albatros. Bowman dived almost to ground level, managed to get his Vickers gun to work and turned to face the enemy scout. Turning to evade Bowman's

In the summer of 1917 No 56 Sqn procured a small boat, fitted it with a motor and Maj Blomfield conducted its first trials. Gerald Maxwell reported, 'Great success. Does about 6 mph'. Here, 'Beery' Bowman, the ever-present pipe firmly clenched, seems a little apprehensive at the expertise of his CO at the tiller

fire, the enemy pilot flew smack into a tree on the edge of Houthulst Forest. Bowman was then attacked by three more Albatros scouts, at which point the plucky RFC pilot decided that had had enough and hedge-hopped back to the British lines, which he crossed at Het Sas at an altitude of just 50 ft.

Bowman's combat report following this eventful action ended with a masterpiece of understatement – 'I then returned to the aerodrome as it was getting late'. However, he confessed to his diary 'Never been so frightened in my life'. The first Albatros he downed was possibly flown by future 33-victory ace Ltn Heinrich Kroll, *Staffelführer* of *Jasta* 24, and the second by Vfw Boldt of the same unit.

The evening engagements of 27 July had been highly successful for No 56 Sqn in general, and Bowman in particular, with the latter being credited with two scouts destroyed – these victories took his tally to 13, six of which had been claimed in July alone. Fellow aces Hoidge and Maybery also claimed single scouts out of control, the latter achieving 'acedom' with this success. On the debit side, Trevor White had been shot down by Oblt Ziegler of *Jasta* 26 and taken prisoner.

In an evening patrol on 28 July, Hoidge first shot down a black and white Albatros, then later, over Roulers, claimed another that was attacking a Camel, the enemy scout going down in pieces. Wilkinson also destroyed an Albatros, its wings 'folding back' as it went down. Hptm Gustav Stenzel of *Jasta* 8 and Ltn Gustav Nolte of *Jasta* 18 were both killed near Rumbeke on this date.

The third Battle of Ypres opened on 31 July. Weather conditions were bad, but this did not deter Richard Maybery from taking off at 0445 hrs to bomb the enemy aerodrome at Heule – home to *Fl Abt* 6, *Fl Abt (A)* 250 and *Jasta* 10. Maybery arrived over the aerodome and circled the field at 200 ft. Other than a man lighting smoke fires at one end, the field was deserted.

David Stanley 'Pud' Wilkinson stands by SE 5 A4853 at Estrée Blanche in late July 1917. This aircraft had previously been flown by C A Lewis, and it still carries his personal markings of white outlined in black around the cockpit area and a red-painted head fairing. The newly issued Camels of No 70 Sqn can be seen in the background

Maybery dropped his first bomb on the sheds at the eastern end of the aerodrome. 'This caused immense excitement', he subsequently recalled. The ace then dropped his second bomb, which landed on the first shed at the southern end. His third bomb exploded inside the final shed, causing smoke to drift out of the doors. Maybery pulled the bomb release to drop his last bomb, but it failed to release and he flew on until he found himself over Courtrai railway station. Maybery pulled the release again, and this time the bomb dropped clear, bursting between a goods train and a shed.

He then returned to the enemy aerodrome, where he was targeted by two machine guns as he flew across the field. Maybery silenced one but failed to spot the other, which wisely ceased firing. He dropped down to 20 ft, fired at the southern sheds, then changed his Lewis gun drum and flew straight across the field from the west, his wheels running along the ground as he fired into the sheds. Zooming for a little height, Maybery flew the short distance to Cuerne, home of *Jasta* 4. Here, he fired at the hangars and sheds – an Albatros scout being wheeled out of one shed was hastily wheeled in again. Leaving the aerodrome, Maybery then attacked two officers on horseback, bolting their mounts.

Turning west, he attacked a train on the Courtrai-to-Menin line, before spotting a column of infantry, 200 strong, marching along the road to Menin. Maybery attacked this column twice, scattering the troops, but then saw a two-seater above him. He zoomed, pulled down his Lewis gun and fired half a drum that sent the enemy machine down to crash on the outskirts of Wevelghem. A crowd gathered around the wreck and Maybery dispersed it, firing both guns. Seeing another locomotive coming from Menin, he dived to attack it, but he was out of Lewis gun ammunition and his Vickers jammed. Maybery returned, having flown no higher than 500 ft during the entire sortie. This action-packed flight was the first bombing attack to be made by a pilot from No 56 Sqn.

Eric Turnbull had taken off 25 minutes after Maybery, with orders to ground strafe targets of opportunity. He attacked transport and troops, but visibility was extremely bad so he returned to Estrée Blanche. By the afternoon it was raining hard, so all flying was abandoned for the day. The bad weather continued for the first four days of August, and the squadron flew no patrols until the afternoon of the 5th, when enemy scouts were engaged. The latter, painted blue and green or blue and yellow, were described as being Albatros fighters, but smaller than usual, with square wingtips and a smaller tail. Barlow shot one of them down, the scout crashing three miles northeast of Dadizele.

The weather turned bad again for the next three days, but patrols were resumed on 9 August. Gordon Ross-Soden was wounded during the last flight of the day, having been set upon by an Albatros. Barlow successfully drove off the enemy scout, but not before Ross-Soden had been hit in the knee. He managed to return to Estrée Blanche, from where he was rushed off to hospital.

10 August saw the unit suffer another casualty. In a fight with Albatros scouts of *Jasta* 6 east of the Menin-to-Roulers road, Wilfred Fleming was shot down and killed by Ltn Stock for his second victory. The last patrol of the day left Estrée Blanche at 1815 hrs. Maybery and Cronyn attacked three Albatros east of Roulers and the former shot one down to crash in a wood to the north of the town. Maybery and Cronyn then attacked

Pages from Verschoyle Philip Cronyn's Royal Aero Club certificate

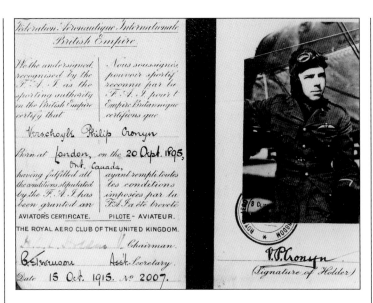

an all-black Albatros. This machine was skilfully handled, but the SE 5s drove it down to 1000 ft and it was subsequently seen to crash just north of Houthulst Forest by Lt Gribben of No 70 Sqn.

Despite being cloudy, with rain, there was a great deal of air fighting on 13 August. Maybery saw an Albatros with a red and black banded fuselage and a yellow tail attacking Leslie Ramage. Maybery drove it off. After fighting several more enemy scouts, he again attacked the yellow-tailed

This triumvirate was know to the squadron as 'The Children'. They are, from left to right, K K Muspratt, A P F Rhys Davids and M H Coote

Albatros, driving it down to 2000 ft. Maybery was now very low over enemy lines so he started to climb, with the yellow-tailed Albatros climbing parallel to him. At 11,000 ft Maybery again attacked and the enemy pilot dived away. Later, over Leke, Maybery and the yellow-tailed machine fought again. Outmanoeuvred, the enemy pilot dived away, but Maybery followed, forcing the Albatros down to 500 ft, where the enemy pilot 'lost' his engine and finally landed east of St Pierre-Capelle 'apparently OK'. Maybery was content with a moral victory.

On the morning of 14 August, Barlow destroyed a two-seater, which crashed in a small wood north of Moorslede, and Muspratt sent another down trailing smoke from its engine. These two-seaters were possibly from *Fl Abt (A)* 224, with Ltn Kamroth being killed in action and his pilot, Gundermann, wounded. *Schusta* 12 had Vfw Kurt Boje wounded and his gunner, Uffz Hermann Hornberger, killed.

During an evening patrol, Maxwell and Robert Sloley sent a large green two-seater down west of Roulers, but as the SE 5s dived away, they were attacked by nine Albatros and 2Lts John Young and Dudley Page were both shot down and taken prisoner. Page later died of his wounds.

During the evening Capt James Byford McCudden arrived to take command of B Flight. McCudden later wrote, 'I don't think I have often experienced such pleasure as when I was able to call myself a flight commander in No 56 Sqn'. McCudden's flight consisted of Arthur Rhys Davids, Leonard Barlow, Keith Muspratt, Maxwell Coote and Canadian Verschoyle Cronyn. McCudden described them 'as splendid a lot of fellows who ever set foot in France'.

Arthur Rhys Davids took the camera from his flight commander in order to take this snapshot of McCudden, flanked by Muspratt and Coote

No 56 Sqn's three flight leaders, Capts J T B McCudden, I H D Henderson and G J C Maxwell. This photo was taken just before Henderson relinquished command of B Flight to McCudden on 15 August 1917. Maxwell led A Flight

Maxwell Henry Coote served with No 56 Sqn from 4 June 1917 until 27 November 1917

Richard Tihel Leighton, who was wounded and then captured on 17 August 1917

The Battle of Langemarck opened on 16 August and the fighter squadrons of the 9th Wing flew continuous close offensive patrols from dawn to dusk. All the flights saw a great deal of fighting, but with no positive result. The next day, over Ypres, Bowman saw an all-red Albatros, which was leading a large formation, dive to attack a balloon that had broken free from its moorings. Richard Leighton later wrote;

'A very large formation of Huns was above us all the time, from 15 to 25. One of them dived on the balloon. They would not fight, despite outnumbering us by more than three-to-one.'

17 August saw some success, but at the cost of two casualties. C Flight was in action with 12 Albatros from *Jasta* 28, led by an all-red machine. Both David Wilkinson and Richard Leighton were shot down, with the latter writing to his mother, Lady Leighton;

'I was brought down on 17 August, I had a fight with several German machines at well over 12,000 ft and all my controls were shot away. I was shot through the top of the shoulder and the side of the forehead, the machine was shot all over too, and came down with a terrific crash in a paddock in the middle of a village eight kilometres behind the German lines. My left arm was broken high up and my forehead badly cut in the crash.'

Leighton survived the war with a steel plate in his head, a memento of 17 August 1917. He had been claimed by Ltn Groos of *Jasta* 11.

David Wilkinson was badly wounded in the back and died of his wounds on 27 August. He was the 23rd victory of Offz Stv Max Müller of *Jasta* 28.

That same evening Barlow shot down an Albatros, the enemy machine falling 'obviously out of control in a series of tumbles'.

18 August saw the end of the Battle of Langemarck. In the morning Maxwell shot down a black and white Albatros near Moorslede, wounding the pilot, Ltn Weinschenk of *Jasta* 18. McCudden sent an Albatros, possibly from *Jasta* 14, down 'in a terrific spiral' which was later confirmed by Barlow. It was McCudden's first victory with the squadron, and his eighth overall.

During the day's fighting, Capt Harold Rushworth was shot down and taken prisoner. He had been attacking a two-seater from *Schusta* 11 when its observer, Uffz Elschenbroich, hit him in the foot and his SE 5 in the petrol tank, engine and rudder bar.

Offz Stv Max Müller of *Jasta* 28 poses with the wreckage of D S Wilkinson's SE 5 A8903 by the side of the canalised River Lys at Bousbecque on 17 August 1917. Wilkinson, who was the Bavarian pilot's 23rd victory, died of his wounds ten days later

Capt James Thomas Byford McCudden joined No 56 Sqn on 15 August 1917, taking command of B Flight. He was the squadron's most successful pilot, scoring 52 of his 57 victories while with the unit

The weather was now very hot. Muspratt wrote home, 'a ripping bath in the afternoon which saved me from dissolving. The heat is appalling, but flying and washing give great relief. Rhys Davids is on leave, so I am all alone, but bearing up'. Next day, over Gheluvelt, McCudden shot down an Albatros marked with red and yellow stripes, and the following evening he downed Vfw Josef Oehler of *Jasta* 24. Oehler's Albatros fell in flames and crashed in a small copse east of Polygon Wood, starting a fire which was still burning an hour later.

Seeing A Flight fighting a group of Albatros, McCudden dived into the engagement and shot at two 'V' Strutters that were attacking an SE 5. Driving off the first, McCudden then closed to within 30 yards of the second, firing a long burst from both guns. The enemy pilot dived, then zoomed. McCudden followed, again firing both guns, and 'continuing to do so until I nearly crashed into his tail. By Jove! It was close'. McCudden did not see the end of this machine, but it was confirmed by Johnston. Barlow was credited with another of the enemy scouts, which went down in a series of 15 spins, and Robert Sloley was also credited with an Albatros out of control.

The following evening, a large patrol of ten SE 5s went to the aid of Bristol Fighters fighting six Albatros 'V' Strutters east of Dixmude. Maxwell later reported;

'SEs spotted enemy formation, dived on them and enemy aircraft made off east. Followed them, some enemy aircraft climbing, some going down. I climbed on to one enemy aircraft's tail, when I noticed an SE (Lt Wilkinson) a long way below over Thourout with two enemy aircraft on his tail and going down rapidly. I therefore dived from 14,000 ft to 5000 ft and got onto the tail of one of the enemy aircraft. He was painted black and white with curious "V" markings around the fuselage. Fired a drum of Lewis and about a hundred rounds of Vickers into him and he stalled, side-slipped and crashed north of Thourout.'

These successes continued on 22 August. The morning sky over Houthulst was 'swarming with enemy scouts', Sloley counting more than 25. The SE 5s attacked the lowest of the enemy formations and Maxwell sent one scout down with smoke pouring from its fuselage – possibly Ltn Auffarrth of *Jasta* 29. Charles Jeffs, in his first action, shot down another of the 'V' Stutters, which crashed near Gheluvelt. The fighting had been very hotly contested, and Maxwell wrote in his diary, 'Splendid scrap. About 40 Huns over Ypres'.

In the evening, McCudden badly damaged a two-seater and Muspratt destroyed another, which fell in a flat spin for 12,000 ft before finally crashing west of Zonnebecke. This machine was from *Fl Abt (A)* 210, and its crew, Ltn d R Albert Wolluhn and Gefr Otto Koch, were both killed.

C Flight also saw a great deal of fighting, Bowman shooting down an Albatros near Roulers, and Maybery, attacking five enemy scouts over Houthulst, sending a green-painted Albatros down to crash near Vierkavenhock. This was possibly Ltn Luer of *Jasta* 27.

22 August had been a highly successful day for No 56 Sqn, as 11 enemy aeroplanes had been brought down. Writing home that night, Muspratt caught the mood of the unit;

'I was out in the evening, there being four from each flight. There was great excitement as the flights' scores were as follows – A had 46 victories, B had 48 victories and C had 47 victories. There was a race to be the first to get 50. I got a two-seater crashed on this side of the lines and one other fellow in B Flight got another two-seater. We are wildly bucked with life and I am all over myself. I am going to try to see the machine I got tomorrow.'

The fine warm weather now gave way to 11 days of rain and strong winds, but offensive patrols continued to be flown nevertheless. On 25 August an evening patrol of six SE 5s fought with seven Albatros 'V' Strutters of *Jasta* 18 two miles east of the frontlines. Jeffs sent one of the enemy scouts 'spinning down' over Roulers and Hoidge fired at a blue Albatros that went down steeply and landed under control east of the Menin-to-Roulers road. This was possibly the aircraft of Ltn Otto Schober of *Jasta* 18.

No further patrols were flown until the last day of the month, when Maxwell and McCudden took their flights out at 1800 hrs. Maxwell led his pilots down to attack eight Albatros scouts circling Moorslede at 12,000 ft. The flight commander's opponent got behind him and hit his SE 5 in the tail. Maxwell struggled to fight back due to stoppages in both guns, and he dived for the cover of the British AA batteries over Ypres, 'chased by a very good red-nosed enemy aircraft who kept on my tail and fired a large number of rounds'. Geoffrey Wilkinson finally shot Vfw Reiss of *Jasta* 3 off Maxwell's tail, the German going down out of control, as confirmed by Lt Taylor of No 66 Sqn.

The continuing rain of the last weeks of the month had turned the ground surrounding the Belgian town of Ypres into a morass. This in turn meant that any ground attacks that were made were purely localised. However, plans were being laid for a resumption of the Ypres offensive as soon as the ground had dried sufficiently, and a heavy programme was being set out for the RFC squadrons to support this campaign.

The Headquarter's Flight pose in the summer of 1917. Only the following individuals have been identified to date – rear row, C P T Davies (extreme left), P P Rossini (third from left), H Fincham (ninth from left) and A Beer (extreme right). Middle row, P C Tomlin (second from left), Capt G Green (third from left), Lt H Charles (fourth from left), A Cox (second from right) and B Beer (extreme right). Front row, S Pegg (extreme left)

OVER THE SALIENT

No 56 Sqn was by now a very formidable fighting unit. In McCudden and Bowman it had two of the finest flight commanders in the RFC, and Gerald Maxwell, despite having no previous combat experience, had also developed into an able flight commander and aggressive fighter.

Other pilots, the raw beginners of a few short months ago, were now experienced and resolute combat veterans, and in Arthur Rhys Davids the squadron considered it had another Ball. Leonard Monteagle Barlow had also fulfilled his early promise. An electrical engineer before the war, Barlow fought with economy and precision, as befits an engineer. Richard Aveline Maybery was a professional soldier. Tall, reserved and modest to a fault, by the end of August 1917 he had become one of the squadron's top scorers with nine victories to his name. The Canadian Reginald Theodore

'Star Turns' of C Flight in the summer of 1917, namely R T C 'Georgie' Hoidge, Geoffrey H 'Beery' Bowman (flight commander) and R A Maybery. Bowman's leg is still bandaged after an accident with a hot exhaust pipe

Carlos Hoidge – nicknamed 'George' – was deputy leader of C Flight. An architect in civilian life, Hoidge was a cheerful extrovert and a magnificent pianist. There were other promising and developing pilots too, but these four men, together with the flight commanders, formed the heart of the squadron.

Weather conditions were changeable during September 1917, but there was a great deal of intense and fiercely contested air fighting nonetheless. Wind, rain and low cloud stopped flying for the first two days of the month, but 3 September was fine and bright. In an evening patrol, Turnbull shot down an Albatros just to the north of Houthulst Forest and Potts stopped the engine of another scout, which went down with its propeller stationary. C Flight was also out, and Maybery destroyed an Albatros that crashed close by the village of Houthem. This scout had also been fired on by both Hoidge and Rhys Davids, and was therefore shared by all three pilots in the squadron's victory lists.

In an evening patrol on 4 September, William Potts shot down Ltn Gebhard Emberger of *Jasta* 29. He jumped from his blazing Albatros and hit the ground on the southern edge of Houthulst Forest.

During an evening patrol on 5 September, C Flight saw a great deal of action. Together with Camels, Nieuports, some FE 2s and Bristol Fighters, the SE 5s attacked eight 'V' Strutters east of Roulers. Rhys Davids shot down one of the enemy scouts, smoke pouring from its engine, before attacking another above him. This scout, which had a red fuselage circled with a black band, dived in front of Rhys Davids. A burst from both guns caused the Albatros to 'wobble' and go steeply down. Rhys Davids then zoomed up and looked back. The scout had broken up, with one wing and the fuselage spinning down very fast, whilst the right wing floated down in small pieces.

For his third victory of the evening, Rhys Davids shot down Vfw Muth of *Jasta* 27. The latter's machine, painted a dull green overall, with a yellow band around the fuselage, crashed a mile northeast of Poelcapelle. Maybery and Hoidge also scored, each claiming a black and white Albatros, and Robert Sloley shot down a two-seater, bringing the total for the evening to six.

Only one patrol was flown on 6 September, but it was notable for providing No 56 Sqn with its first sighting of two German enemy scouts – the Fokker Dr I triplane and the Pfalz D III. An early morning patrol, led by McCudden, sighted the enemy force, which included a Pfalz (described as a 'Fokker biplane') and two Fokker triplanes. Sloley attacked the Pfalz, which dived under the cover of its companions. One of the triplane pilots fired a long-range burst at Sloley as he turned away, but came no nearer. Sloley commented that the pilot of the triplane 'showed little determination in spite of a very favourable position'. Leaving this formation, the SE 5s later attacked two 'V' Strutters and Jeffs shot one down to crash just east of Poelcapelle railway station.

Weather conditions halted all flying until 9 September, when an evening patrol saw a great deal of incident. Turnbull and Potts collided in mid-air, but luckily neither SE 5 was badly damaged and they returned safely. Rhys Davids experienced several indecisive brushes with enemy scouts, the ace being frustrated by gun troubles. He eventually joined up with Sloley and attacked an Albatros, Rhys Davids' fire hitting the fighter in the cockpit and centre section – smoke and boiling water poured out of its radiator prior to the scout crashing in Houthulst Forest. This success took Rhys Davids' tally to 19 victories, five of which had come in September alone.

On 10 September Potts and Hoidge claimed enemy scouts out of control and Maybery destroyed a red-nosed Albatros, which went down with one wing breaking away from the fuselage. It hit the ground southeast of Houthulst Forest. Although the German lists, as they so often do, show no loss for the day, it is hard to see how the pilot of this Albatros could have survived.

A morning patrol the following day saw No 56 Sqn tangle with *Jasta* 7. During the melee, which included Naval triplanes, high-scoring ace and *Staffelführer* Ltn Josef Jacobs hit Rhys Davids' SE 5 in the gravity petrol tank, forcing him to return. McCudden fought ace Obfg Kurt Schönfelder of the *Jasta* down over Zonnebecke, but realising that he was now very low over enemy territory, he broke off the action. During the evening patrol, Hoidge shot down a scout from a formation of six and later wounded the observer in a two-seater before the pilot dived east, smoke pouring from the engine of his aircraft.

This was a day of considerable frustration for the squadron's pilots, as only two victories had been scored and many good tactical positions had been wasted by continuous gun troubles. McCudden summed up the general disgust in a letter to his father;

'This morning I got 20 yards behind a Hun, took a sight on the back of his neck and pulled the triggers but neither gun fired a single shot. While I was rectifying the stoppages the Hun got away.'

The next victories were not claimed until 14 September. Eight Albatros were seen over Zandvoorde, with Sloley shooting down one out of control and Lts Jeffs and Horrell each claiming another. Bowman made no mistake with his victim. Following his opponent into a cloud, he emerged with the Albatros just 100 yards in front of him. Bowman closed to 'very close range', and 30 rounds sent the enemy scout down to crash a mile northeast of Menin. On the debit side, Hoidge had been shot down. A burst of fire had hit his SE 5 in the engine and he force-landed, unhurt, north of Zillebecke Lake.

In the evening B Flight was in action with *Jasta* 11 over Roulers. McCudden wounded Oblt Weigand, hitting his machine in the engine. The Albatros began to vibrate badly, but Weigand managed to land the damaged fighter. Rhys Davids attacked another Albatros, flown by Ltn Groos, and sent it down with smoke pouring from its engine. In a later action, over Menin, Rhys Davids was outmanoeuvred by an enemy pilot flying an Albatros with a green fuselage and silver tail. The enemy pilot, possibly Ltn Julius Schmidt of *Jasta* 3, hit the SE 5 in the petrol tank. Rhys Davids flew west and landed at Bailleul. Norman Crow failed to return, however, having been shot down and killed by Ltn Karl Menckhoff of *Jasta* 3 for his 11th victory.

The usual strong formation of two flights took off on the evening of 16 September. B Flight went to the aid of a formation of SE 5s from No 60 Sqn that were fighting with Albatros scouts – possibly from *Jasta* 17 – over Houthem. McCudden watched Barlow finishing off an Albatros 'in great style', the enemy scout crashing near Wervicq.

Norman Howard Crow was killed in action on 14 September 1917

No flying was possible for the next two days, but on the 19th McCudden took off at 1030 hrs 'to look for two-seaters'. He first attacked a DFW, which dived away so steeply that several objects fell out of it. Thirty-five minutes later, McCudden attacked a Rumpler over Estaires, which he shot down one mile behind the German lines at Radinghem.

The Battle of the Menin Ridge road opened on the morning of 20 September. Maxwell and Sloley attacked a two-seater over Wervicq and it went down with its engine smoking – Maxwell estimated that it would crash just east of Ypres. All the flights saw a good deal of fighting during the day, but with no decisive results. On the ground, good progress was being made, the troops aided by the valuable work of the RFC squadrons, whose observations gave early warnings of German counter-attacks forming up.

Maxwell was the next pilot to score. On 21 September, he destroyed a two-seater in flames (for his 17th victory overall), the aircraft crashing into a wood near Verlinghem. Uffzs Krause and Schieber of *Fl Abt (A) 227* were both killed. During this engagement, however, Lt William Potts had been shot down and killed by Ltns Haack and Klostermann, also of *Fl Abt (A) 227*. Maxwell entered in his diary, 'Saw Potts crash. Wings folded up in air'.

William Janson Potts was killed in action on 21 September 1917

Ten SE 5s left Estrée Blanche at 1645 hrs that same afternoon, one of the aircraft being flown by Cronyn. He later recorded in his diary, 'I had never seen so many Huns before. There must have been about 60 altogether, and only about ten were two-seaters'. The SE 5s attacked the two-seaters, without success, but Hoidge destroyed a scout that broke up in mid-air. Cronyn's diary recorded, 'The Huns are very much more cautious than they were three weeks ago'.

LEGENDARY COMBAT

23 September was to see a combat that has become an epic in the annals of air fighting. A combined force of 11 SE 5as left the ground at 1700 hrs. McCudden first destroyed a two-seater, which crashed at Houthem, killing Ltn Rudolph and Uffz Franke of *Fl Abt 6*. A little later, McCudden and his flight were about to attack a formation of Albatros scouts when they saw an SE 5 under attack from a triplane. 'The SE certainly looked very unhappy, so we changed our minds about attacking the "V" Strutters and went to the rescue of the unfortunate SE'.

The SE 5 in question was being flown by No 60 Sqn ace Capt Harold Hamersley, who had made the mistake of attacking the Fokker Dr I of 48-victory ace Ltn Werner Voss, *Staffelführer* of *Jasta 10*. The German had easily out-manoeuvred Hamersley and badly damaged his SE 5. Fellow ace Capt Robert Chidlaw-Roberts of No 60 Sqn had attempted to come to Hamersley's aid, but he too had been severely handled by Voss, who shot his rudder bar to pieces.

McCudden attacked the triplane from the right and Rhys Davids from the left. Voss saw them coming and turned, 'in a most disconcertingly quick manner – not a climbing or Immelmann turn, but a sort of flat half spin'. C Flight had now joined in the fight, and Voss was in the middle of eight SE 5as. Nevertheless, he evaded all attempts to give any of the pilots a decisive shot. Voss sent both Cronyn and Muspratt out of the fight, the latter with only a damaged radiator, but Cronyn's machine was so badly damaged that it was later written off.

Ltn Werner Voss was shot down on the evening of 23 September 1917 after an epic fight with elements of B and C Flights. McCudden later wrote of him 'He is the bravest German airman whom it has been my privilege to see fight'

Although Voss was now fighting some of the RFC's most experienced pilots, he made no attempt to break off the action, Maybery reporting that 'he seemed invulnerable'. However, such an uneven fight could have only one outcome, and Rhys Davids finally got a good burst of Vickers and Lewis into the triplane before zooming away. When he saw it next the Fokker Dr I was gliding west. Rhys Davids dived and attacked again, but overshot. Voss made a right hand turn and went down. Rhys Davids failed to see the end of the triplane, but both Bowman and McCudden saw it crash just inside the British frontlines. This epic fight had lasted ten minutes. The time was now between 1835 hrs and 1840 hrs, and the No 56 Sqn pilots returned home.

There was a great deal of speculation in the Mess that evening as to the identity of the German pilot who had fought so magnificently. News came later that it had been Werner Voss. He had crashed at Plum Farm, just north of Frezenberg.

On 24 September, three enemy two-seaters were seen returning from the British side of the lines, evidently having successfully photographed the Allied rear areas. It was imperative that these machines should not get back to their airfields with their photographs, and B Flight attacked them. Rhys Davids tackled a machine from *Fl Abt (A)* 256 and shot it down in flames, killing Ltns Carl von Esmarch and Hans Fleischer. Barlow destroyed another, which crashed into the trees of Houthulst Forest. The third machine made it home, however.

The following day dawned fine and bright. In the afternoon, Barlow attacked two Albatros and two Pfalz D IIIs from *Jasta* 10 over Houthulst Forest. Oblt Weingard's Albatros went down in pieces before bursting into flames. Barlow then attacked a Pfalz flown by Uffz Werkmeister, and this too went down and crashed at Stampkot. He then turned his attention to the remaining 'V' Strutters, shooting one down to crash half-a-mile from the northwest corner of the forest. Its pilot escaped with his life, but Weingard and Werkmeister were both killed.

On 26 September, Maxwell and his flight had an indecisive combat with AEG G IV bombers. Maxwell commented in his diary, 'Saw and attacked 11 Gothas over the lines east of Ypres. Got underneath one and fired a lot of rounds, but Gotha did not notice at all. Played soccer in the evening with men. Draw'.

The next day McCudden shot down a two-seater from *Schusta* 27 for his 14th victory. The pilot, Uffz Gossler, fell within the British lines, but the observer, Uffz Wiedermann, landed in his own lines. Both men were killed. McCudden scored again the next day, shooting an Albatros from *Jasta* 29 to pieces over Houthulst Forest. Its pilot, Ltn Pastor, fell clear of his machine. In this action, Barlow also sent an Albatros down in a steep dive, sliding from side to side. Rhys Davids later attacked five 'V' Strutters, one of which turned into his line of fire and went down vertically with two columns of smoke pouring out of its engine. There is a distinct possibility that this machine was flown by Oblt Herman Göring, *Staffelführer* of *Jasta* 27. If so, it is interesting to speculate on just how different the course of history may have been had Rhys Davids' fire been more accurate.

A and C Flights took off at 1630 hrs. Hoidge and Bowman kept just above the clouds, and at 1720 hrs a pair of 'V' Strutters 'cautiously'

This shot of Gerald Maxwell, A Flight Commander, taxiing out at Estrée Blanche in the early autumn of 1917 was taken by James McCudden, his fellow flight commander

E R Taylor, D J Reason, H A Johnston and A P F Rhys Davids pose for the camera at Estrée Blanche in September 1917

poked their noses into the clear sky. Bowman and Hoidge shot down both scouts, Hoidge's opponent falling into the forest one mile east of Westroosebeke. Bowman's diary commented, 'Got one "V" Strutter. Broke up in air after 4000 ft. First enemy aircraft of mine to be seen to break up. Splendid'. These Albatros were from *Jasta* 3, the unit having Ltn Kurt Wissemann killed over Westroosebeke on this date.

Maxwell shot down an Albatros east of Houthulst Forest on 28 September, the enemy scout being seen to break up by Ralph Young. Maxwell and Johnston were each awarded a scout victory following this patrol, and a third was credited to the whole flight.

On the last day of the month, No 56 Sqn scored its 200th aerial victory, as already detailed at the start of chapter one. In many ways this event was to act as the swansong for the original unit that had flown to France from England in April.

Despite adverse weather conditions that curtailed flying for no fewer than 12 days, October was to be a bad month for the squadron. Six pilots were killed in action, one fatally wounded and another taken prisoner. Included in the casualties were some of the squadron's best and most promising pilots.

1 October was bright and cloudless. McCudden attacked a Rumpler over Merville, wounding the observer. The enemy pilot dived away, McCudden following. Another full drum of Lewis caused smoke to pour from the Rumpler, and it went down over Herlies. A patrol in the afternoon saw the first casualty of the month. During a large combat, involving SE 5as of A and B Flights, some Bristol Fighters and 20 Albatros scouts, McCudden saw an SE 5 fighting four 'V' Strutters. One of the enemy scouts managed to get onto the tail of the RFC fighter and shot its wings off from a range of just 25 yards. 'It was poor Sloley, who was, as usual, where the Huns were thickest'. South African 2Lt Robert Sloley had claimed eight victories prior to his demise. Two Albatros were claimed from this fight, with one being credited to Rhys Davids and the other to B Flight as a whole.

Maxwell's diary summed up the events of the following morning – 'Plenty of scrapping'. He attacked a two-seater and killed the observer,

Robert Hugh Sloley was killed in action on 1 October 1917

who was lying over the side of his cockpit, 'obviously dead', but then lost sight of the enemy machine. C Flight was also out, fighting a formation of 'V' Strutters over Moorslede. Maybery fired both guns into one before zooming away, Bowman seeing the scout crash half-a-mile from St Pieter. Ltn Max Roemer of *Jasta* 10 was killed in the crash. In a later fight with a large formation of black and white Albatros, Gilbert and Gardiner were both roughly handled by their German opponents, leaving their SE 5s badly damaged.

B and C Flights went out again in the evening, but from the outset they were in a bad tactical position. Bowman's logbook contains the caustic comment, 'Driven out of sky twice'. B Flight had better luck, Muspratt attacking an Albatros. 'I opened fire at 50 yards and must have hit him with my first shots, as I saw his machine quiver and he kept going straight on'. Muspratt continued firing and the Albatros went down vertically. 'He must have been unconscious as he passed close by many of our machines without firing, and they all thought he was dead. However, he flattened out quite close to the ground and went for home. He won't fight again for a bit'. Muspratt then 'had a difference' with three enemy scouts, one of which was a triplane, but when he was joined by Rhys Davids the enemy fighters cleared east.

Low clouds and rain stopped flying for the next two days. On 5 October there was a great deal of fighting over the hamlet of America, however. Reginald Preston-Cobb's SE 5a was badly shot up, forcing him to land near Caestre, and Charles Jeffs became the 13th victim of Oblt Bruno Loerzer, *Staffelführer* of *Jasta* 26 – Jeffs survived as a PoW.

By now the weather had turned very cold, and the pilots woke to the welcome sound of rain on their tents on 6 October. The poor weather would persist for four days. News reached No 56 Sqn during this time that both Barlow and McCudden had been awarded second Bars to their MCs, and a celebratory dinner was duly held in the Mess.

Although the weather was still wet, patrols resumed once again on 10 October. In an afternoon combat with elements of *Jastas* 18 and 26, Geoffrey Wilkinson was shot down and killed by Ltn Danhuber of *Jasta* 26. Maxwell wrote 'saw Wilkinson go down in pieces with a Hun on his tail'. Maxwell in turn fired from 'very close range' into one of the 'V' Strutters, which dived steeply away. His victim was possibly high-scoring ace Oblt Rudolf Berthold of *Jasta* 18, who was badly wounded when a bullet shattered his right arm on 10 October .

Although the bad weather continued on 11 October, a morning patrol of six SE 5s fought twelve enemy scouts – a mixed bag of 'V' Strutters and Pfalz D IIIs. During the fighting, McCudden, with both his guns being out of action, fired his Very pistol at a Pfalz, hoping to panic the pilot. Additional 'V' Strutters now joined in the fight, resulting in Preston-Cobb being shot down and killed by Ltn Hoyer of *Jasta* 36 and James Cunningham suffering serious wounds to his back. The latter pilot force landed at Pont-de-Nieppe and was rushed to hospital, but he subsequently died of his wounds.

The next positive success for No 56 Sqn was not achieved until 17 October. Over Poelcapelle Bowman attacked a two-seater, zooming up underneath it and firing 50 rounds from his Vickers. The SE 5a then stalled, and when Bowman recovered he saw a long streak of smoke against the sky, with 'the enemy aircraft at the end of it'.

Charles Hugh Jeffs became a PoW on 5 October 1917

Jeffs (right) is seen here after capture with his victor, Oblt Bruno Loerzer, *Staffelführer* of *Jasta* 26. Loerzer is wearing a British leather flying coat, much prized by German pilots

McCudden also shot down an LVG C V on this date, its centre section bursting into flames and the observer standing up in an attitude of 'abject dejection'. The fire went out, but it had burnt most of the fabric off the LVG's rudder. Muspratt and Barlow now arrived, and spotting that the flames had been extinguished, they both attacked the enemy machine. The LVG went into a dive, both of its wings broke off and the aircraft crashed just south of Vlamertinghe.

By the time McCudden had landed alongside the wreckage, Australian troops had gathered around the remains of the observer, who had fallen out of his machine at 5000 ft. 'He was a huge man named Ernst Hädrich', the ace later recalled. McCudden's disciplined mind was horrified by the unedifying behaviour of the antipodean troops, who swarmed all over the remains of the LVG, stripping it of anything of value, including the clothing of the observer, and Blomfield later submitted an official report. This LVG, from *Fl Abt* 8, was McCudden's 17th victory. Both crewmen – Oblt Hädrich and Flg Horstmann – had been killed.

On the morning of 18 October, after a fight with several highly coloured Albatros scouts (all with yellow noses and tails, and one with a tail 'chequered like a draughts board'), Hoidge shot down a two-seater, which crashed near Comines. He then attacked another two-seater, but left it to go to the aid of Lt John Gilbert who was under attack from a persistent 'V' Strutter. Both Gilbert and Geoffrey Shone failed to return. Gilbert was shot down and killed by Ltn Ernst Udet of *Jasta* 37, the RFC pilot being his 14th victim. Shone, shot down in flames by Vfw Kampe of *Jasta* 27, crashed behind the British lines near St Julien and died of his wounds the following day.

On 21 October, the 9th Wing HQ telephoned No 56 Sqn and ordered that it intercept three enemy two-seaters that were heading south from Calais. McCudden, Rhys Davids and Muspratt took off, but they saw only a DH 4. Although Rhys Davids and Muspratt returned home, McCudden stayed, climbing for more height. Once over Bethune, he saw a Rumpler above him. The enemy pilot also spotted the SE 5a and dived away to the east, although McCudden felt sure that he would return,

A Flight in the autumn of 1917. Only the following individuals have been identified to date – back row, W Milton (second from left), G Devis (third from right), J Allen (second from right) and F H Pitt (extreme right). Middle row, J Charles (first from left), A H Rix (third from left), W Ferguson (fourth from left), E A Clements (fifth from left), E W Ellison (fifth from right), A W Hale (third from right), R J Davis (second from right) and P E Wicks (extreme right). And front row, L G Baker (extreme left), F Brittain (third from left), H B Pickett (fourth from left), flight commander Capt Hoidge (centre), A Eastes (fourth from right), C Gibson (third from right), Reggitt (second from right) and A Briggs (extreme right)

McCudden poses in SE 5a B4863 outside the B Flight hangars at Estrée Blanche

Arthur Percival Foley Rhys Davids was killed in action on 27 October 1917. McCudden wrote of him, 'If one was ever over the Salient in the autumn of 1917 and saw an SE 5 fighting like Hell amidst a heap of Huns, one would find nine times out of ten that the SE was flown by Rhys Davids'

so he carefully hoarded his height. After a long chase, McCudden finally engaged the Rumpler over Bethune once again. The two-seater went down in a spin, 'emitting clouds of steam', and hit the ground near Mazingarbe. McCudden landed nearby. The observer, Ltn Laito, was dead, and the pilot, Uffz Hiltweis, lived for only a few moments more. This Rumpler C IV (8431/16) was from *Fl Abt* 5.

Low clouds prevented any flying from taking place on 23 October, so McCudden went on leave. With Gerald Maxwell and Leonard Barlow posted to Home Establishment, plus the recent casualties, there suddenly seemed to be a great number of new faces in No 56 Sqn.

The morning patrol on 23 October – a mixed force of pilots from B and C Flights – was to have a tragic outcome. After an indecisive fight with two Pfalz D IIIs and six 'V' Strutters, Bowman and two other SE 5as attacked a group of enemy scouts two miles west of Iseghem. Bowman sent one down in a spin before the enemy formation scattered and dived away to the east. Arthur Rhys Davids failed to return from this patrol.

At first there was no anxiety. It was felt, as Bowman later recalled, 'it would have to be a damned good Hun to get "RD"'. However, as the day progressed with no news, it became clear that Rhys Davids was down on the other side. He had been shot down and killed by Ltn Karl Gallwitz of *Jasta* 'Boelcke' for his fifth victory. The squadron had not suffered such a heavy blow since the loss of Ball. Just 20 years of age, Rhys Davids, who had claimed 25 victories prior to his demise, had many friends in the RFC and was extremely popular, thus making his loss even more keenly felt. Rhys Davids has no known grave and is commemorated on the Air Services Memorial at Arras.

On the morning of 28 October, Maybery was attacked by an Albatros whose wings and tailplane were adorned with black and green stripes. The enemy pilot overshot and Maybery fired his Lewis as it went by. The

No 56 Sqn COs Majs Rainsford Balcombe Brown (left) and Richard Graham Blomfield stand outside the squadron office in late October 1917. This photograph was taken to record the moment when Blomfield handed over command to Balcombe Brown. The famous sign on the office door reads 'Officer Commanding. Enter without knocking'. All credit must go, of course, to Maj Blomfield for laying the foundations of the squadron's successes in 1917, but he never flew in action with the unit. Indeed, it was officially forbidden for commanding officers to do so. Consequently, Blomfield was a rather distant figure to those pilots who had joined the squadron in late 1917. In fact they found some of his mannerisms and morale boosting schemes rather irritating. Balcombe Brown was a fine pilot, and he was the only CO of the squadron to be killed on active service. However, his manner was inclined to be supercilious, and he was rather scathing in his remarks to pilots on their flying abilities – 'try to land on the World the next time' was his favourite comment on a bad landing, perhaps made under some stress. Unfortunately, these tendencies cost him the liking and respect of some of the pilots. Nevertheless, he commanded the squadron through perhaps its hardest period of duty

Albatros went down with its engine still full on, and it was seen to crash near Dadizele.

Muspratt took B Flight out the following morning, and it attacked nine Albatros 'V' Strutters southwest of Roulers. Muspratt went after a scout that was flying a streamer from each elevator, and his fire caused the left hand side of its tailplane to completely crumple up. Maxwell Coote shot down another of the 'V' Strutters, which was confirmed by Harry Slingsby. The patrol's combat reports were countersigned for the first time by the No 56 Sqn's new commanding officer, Maj Rainsford Balcombe Brown.

Later that same day Bowman shot down a Pfalz D III, which crashed near the railway line to the north of Moorslede. He also wounded the observer in a two-seater. A farewell dinner for Maj Richard Blomfield rounded out the day. 'Everything was the same except Rhys Davids was not there', Bowman recalled.

Low clouds and rain stopped all flying on 30 October. The next day, after several indecisive combats, Maybery finally scored, shooting down an Albatros that fell away with smoke pouring from it. This machine was possibly flown by Uffz Reinhold of *Jasta* 24, who was wounded in action on 31 October. Later in the morning, Keith Muspratt shot down a two-seater that crashed into a row of trees near Stadenberg.

The afternoon saw a furious fight between A and C Flights and enemy scouts southwest of Roulers. Hoidge forced one Albatros down out of control and Herbert Johnston sent another – painted black and white – over onto its back before it went down in a spin, finishing in a steep dive. Maybery fired at a red and yellow Albatros, almost certainly flown by ace Ltn Erwin Böhme, *Staffelführer* of *Jasta* 'Boelcke', who evaded his attack. The latter then shot down a black and blue Albatros that crash-landed in a large field. Maybery was now very low, and Böhme got in a good burst at close range, hitting the SE 5 in the petrol tank and stopping the engine. Maybery went down, looking for a place to land, then, remembering his emergency fuel tank, switched it on. His engine restarted and he managed to return home.

This combined patrol of A and C Flights was the last flown in October. It had been a bad month for No 56 Sqn, but with the prospect of the winter weather, and its slackening of activity, there would be time to retrench and train the new pilots.

Low clouds and rain kept the squadron on the ground for the first seven days of November. During a patrol on the 8th, in a fight with black and white Albatros scouts over Moorslede, Felix Cobbold was shot down by Ltn Fritz Loerzer of *Jasta* 28 for his fifth victory – Cobbald survived as a PoW. A second patrol brought another casualty for no gains when Capt Phillip Cowan was shot down and killed by Ltn Hans von Habler of *Jasta* 36.

There was no further flying until 13 November, when the squadron moved to a new aerodrome at Laviéville, near Albert. The unit was now under the command of the 13th Wing, being added to its strength for the coming Battle of Cambrai. In view of the impending onset of winter, the move was welcomed, for instead of the tents at Estrée Blanche, pilots and groundcrew were now housed in Nissen huts and the aeroplanes in iron hangars.

Felix Cobbold's SE 5a B630 came down behind German lines on 8 November 1917. Cobbold had been wounded and shot down by Ltn Fritz Loerzer of *Jasta* 26, the brother of Bruno Loerzer, the *Staffelführer*

The first patrol on the new front took off on 18 November. McCudden duly shot down an LVG, which crashed into a trench, for his 19th victory. Later that same morning Lt John Waters was killed while testing an SE 5a, his machine breaking up at 1000 ft. The next day Reginald Hoidge was posted to Home Establishment, leaving only Gerald Constable Maxwell of the original pilots who had flown to France with No 56 Sqn seven months earlier.

The unit's orders for the Battle of Cambrai were Deep Offensive Patrols, but while their less fortunate compatriots in the Camel and DH 5 squadrons were ground strafing, suffering a casualty rate of 30 per cent, bad weather kept No 56 Sqn on the ground.

The morning of 23 November was overcast, but conditions were improving, and McCudden took out B Flight at 1040 hrs. Over Cambrai, he attacked the leader of four Albatros scouts. This aircraft had a green tail, a red nose, yellow fuselage and a letter 'K' on its top wing. This was the first appearance of 'Greentail', as the Albatros was nicknamed – an aircraft that was to be met many times over the coming months by pilots from No 56 Sqn. No results were gained from this fight, but McCudden later shot down an Albatros, the enemy machine hitting the ground with

Eric Leslie Lowe Turnbull was the commander of A Flight from 19 December 1917 through to 26 January 1918

'a fearful whack' between Noyelles and Rumilly. This was possibly Offz Stv Karl Bey of *Jasta* 5, who was killed.

Maybery and A Flight were also out that day, diving on a two-seater. Burdette Harmon forced the enemy machine down and it overturned on landing. The pilot, from *Fl Abt* 25, was uninjured, but the observer, Ltn d R Erich Herold, perished.

In the afternoon, 'Beery' Bowman shot down a brown-coloured Albatros, which crashed just northeast of Cambrai. There had been a great deal of fighting on the 23rd for very little positive result, and Maj Balcombe Brown returned home with his SE 5a badly damaged. Attacking an enemy two-seater, he had turned the wrong way and his scout was hit in the petrol tank by the enemy gunner's fire. Balcombe Brown ruefully remarked that shooting down a two-seater was harder than it looked.

There were no further successes until the morning of 29 November, when McCudden attacked a DFW over Bellincourt and literally shot it to pieces, the fuselage hitting the ground south of the village. This aircraft, from *Fl Abt (A)* 202, was crewed by Ltn d Rs Kurt Dettrich and Manfred Hoettger.

Maybery and his flight were also in action, fighting Albatros scouts. He sent one down out of control and Eric Turnbull's opponent turned over onto its side and spiralled down in a slow spin. These fighters were from *Jasta* 5, records showing that the unit's Albatros D V 2082/17 crashed on landing after a combat at 1020 hrs. The pilot was unhurt. During this clash Lt Alexander Dodds was shot down and taken prisoner. He had been attacked by Ltn Schubert of *Jasta* 6 and forced to land at *Jasta* 5's aerodrome at Boistrancourt.

In an afternoon patrol, McCudden shot down another DFW that shed all four of its wings prior to the fuselage hitting the ground near Rouvroy. The crew, Ltn d R Georg Dietrich and Ltn Deitrich Schenk, of *Fl Ab (A)*

Ltns Schlömer (left) and Oppenhorst with Alexander Dodds' SE 5a B4890. On 29 November 1917, Dodds was forced to land on the aerodrome of *Jasta* 5 at Boistrancourt by Ltn Schubert of *Jasta* 6

268 were both killed. Harold Walkerdine shot down a companion two-seater, which crashed at Neuvireuil.

On 30 November, McCudden continued his success with two-seaters by shooting down an LVG of *Fl Abt* 19. This LVG landed relatively unscathed in the British lines, and McCudden, his radiator having been hit by fire from the observer, landed nearby – the SE 5a hit a shell hole and ended up on its nose. McCudden pulled down the scout's tail and hurried over to the LVG. The pilot, Vfw Flohrig, was badly wounded and died on his way to hospital, but the observer, Gefr Eckerle was unhurt. This LVG C V 9458/17 was given the RFC number G 94.

Later that day Maybery attacked a two-seater, but he had to turn away when his guns jammed. George Cawson then attacked the machine, but accurate return fire from the enemy gunner caused his SE 5a to break up and he was killed. Cawson was credited to Vfws Voigt and Kruse of *Schusta* 12, who were ultimately forced to land. Maybery had better luck during an afternoon patrol, shooting down an Albatros which crashed, engine full on, west of Bourlon Wood. He then attacked another scout, which exploded and broke up under his fire. This was possibly Ltn Johann von Senger of *Jasta* 12. The day was ended by Bowman shooting down a Pfalz D III, which crashed by the canal at Cantaing. This machine was possibly flown by Ltn d R Friedrich Demandt of *Jasta* 10.

In a later patrol, Maurice Mealing shot an Albatros down out of control, but three others attacked Ronald Townsend, whose SE 5a burst into flames at 1000 ft. The RFC pilot was claimed by Vfw Josef Mai of *Jasta* 5 as his fifth victory. Townsend was the last of six pilots lost by No 56 Sqn during November, and although they were all relatively inexperienced, it could ill afford such losses.

Despite weather conditions ruling out flying for a number of days in December, there was still a great deal of intense and fiercely contested fighting during the month. Although hampered by strong winds, patrols were flown on 2 December, but the adverse conditions caused several pilots to crash upon returning to Laviéville.

Just after 1100 hrs on 5 December, McCudden took off alone to look for high-flying Rumplers. While at 19,000 ft over Havrincourt Wood, he saw a two-seater coming west at the same height. Waiting until the Rumpler was well west of the British lines, McCudden finally attacked it over Boursies. 'I very quickly secured a good firing position, and after firing a burst from both guns, the Rumpler went down in a vertical dive. All of its wings fell off at 16,000 ft and the wreckage came down in our lines near Hermies'. This Rumpler, from *Fl Abt* 45, was crewed by Ltns Pauly and Sauter, both of whom were killed.

Later in the day, Bowman attempted to shoot down a balloon, but he dived so enthusiastically that three wings spars of his SE 5a snapped. He flew home as fast as he dared, anxiously watching the wingtips, 'which were wobbling about like jelly'.

Maybery and a young Indian pilot by the name of Lt Indra Roy were the first pilots to take off on 6 December, and they duly went to the aid of Bristol Fighters that were being attacked by seven 'V' Strutters. Maybery's opponent had a light blue tail, and he reported that the enemy pilot was 'very good'. Maybery eventually hit this Albatros in the engine but was driven off by its companions before he could finish the scout off. B Flight

Richard Aveline Maybery was killed in action on 19 December 1917. Hearing of Maybery's death, Blomfield wrote, 'Capt Maybery was, I think, the bravest and most dashing air fighter I have ever come across'

had taken off five minutes after Maybery and Roy, and McCudden shot down another Rumpler in his usual workmanlike manner. At 8000 ft the wings came off the enemy machine, and it hit the ground near Holnon Wood. Ltn Becker and Uffz Pohlisch of *Fl Abt* 255 were both killed.

After lunch B Flight fought a patrol from *Jasta* 5. McCudden sent one Albatros, sporting a light blue tail, down in a vertical dive, petrol pouring from its fuselage, and Mealing claimed another, leaving its engine smoking. However, these German pilots proved to be worthy foes, McCudden commenting, 'By Jove! They were a tough lot. We continued scrapping with them for half-an-hour, and they would not go down, although we were above them most of the time'.

The next patrols were not flown until 10 December. In the afternoon, both Bowman and Leslie Franklin claimed scouts out of control, whilst McCudden shot a two-seater in the radiator and Maurice Mealing downed a balloon in flames. On 12 December, after dispersing some Pfalz D IIIs that were ground strafing British troops, McCudden attacked a DFW, but found it more than he could handle. 'The enemy aircraft put up a most determined and skilful fight, and I was not able to use his blind spots for a single second. Moreover, the enemy gunner was shooting very accurately and making splendid deflection'. McCudden finally left this determined German crew at 500 ft over Bourlon Wood. He admitted, 'The Hun was too good for me and shot me about a lot. Had I persisted he certainly would have got me, for there was not a trick he did not know'.

Bad weather kept the squadron on the ground until 15 December, when two victories were scored. Maybery sent a red-nosed Albatros down in a spin, then attacked another. 'Something large fell off the fuselage of the enemy aircraft fuselage and he went into a slow left hand turn, then nose-dived for 2000 ft, then flattened out'.

McCudden took off alone at 1020 hrs. 'By the time I got to our lines the whole sky seemed alive with two-seaters'. He attacked one of these, a Rumpler, north of Gonnelieu. It went into a spiral dive for 5000 ft, finally hitting the ground half-a-mile east of Bois-de-Vaycelles. 'Nothing was left of it'. This was McCudden's 27th victory.

The next patrols were not flown until 19 December, when Maybery and McCudden took their flights out at 1215 hrs. In confused fighting with several formations of enemy scouts, Turnbull saw an Albatros going down in flames with an SE 5a – which Turnbull took to be Maybery – on its tail. Blenkiron shot at another enemy scout and black smoke poured out of the fuselage under the pilot's seat, the Albatros rolling over onto its back. On return to Laviéville it was realised that Richard Maybery had not been seen since the attack on the enemy scouts over Bourlon Wood. He had been shot down by *K-Flakbatterie* 108, commanded by a Ltn Thiel, and was buried 600 yards south of the village of Haynecourt, by the side of the road to Sailly.

With 21 victories to his name, Richard Maybery was a great loss to the squadron. He had been due to go home to England within the next few weeks, as Bowman later recalled. 'Richard was tired, and I asked him to take my Leave. I was still fresh, didn't need it and was only going to Paris anyway. He wouldn't hear of it, and I never saw him again'.

On the morning of 22 December, McCudden attacked a pair of DFW two-seaters crossing the lines over Maissemy. His fire stopped the engine

Maybery tests the engine of SE 5a B4880. He collected this machine from No 2 Aeroplane Supply Depot and had it marked with the flight commander's letter, but on 19 December 1917 the scout's engine was 'not running very well'. Maybery hastily switched to SE 5a B506, and he was killed whilst at its controls

of the first and McCudden left it gliding down in the British lines, turning his attentions to its companion. The enemy crew put up a stiff fight for their lives and McCudden finally left the machine over St Quentin, having failed to gain a decisive result. He then saw that the first DFW had turned east and was gliding down to land on its own side of the lines. McCudden turned back, fired a short burst, and the DFW, from *Schusta* 5, crashed in British-held territory half-a-mile behind the frontline trenches near St Quentin. The G report on this DFW mentions only Uffz Anton Bode as the pilot, who was killed, but the records of *Schusta* 5 reveal that Bode was the gunner, and the pilot, Uffz Bisenbach, was taken prisoner.

McCudden again took off alone of 23 December. It was to be a day of remarkable success. His first victory, an LVG, crashed between the canal and the road at Anguilcourt. Five minutes later McCudden saw a Rumpler from *Fl Abt* 23, crewed by Ltns Höring and Tibussek. An accurate burst from McCudden's guns at 8000 ft over Roupy shot the starboard wings off the aircraft, the wreckage falling in the British lines near Contescourt.

McCudden took his flight out in the afternoon, and within 30 minutes he had spotted yet another Rumpler over Metz-en-Couture. A long burst sent this aircraft down to crash in the British lines northwest of Gouzeaucourt. The crew, from *Bogohl* 7, were taken prisoner. After a fight with 'Greentail's' flight of Albatros 'V' Strutters, McCudden next had an LVG pointed out to him by British 'Archie'. After a short burst, the LVG 'stalled and spun, and after that it went down just like a leaf – it took at least three minutes to crash. It landed on a light gauge train in a vertical

dive and knocked some trucks off the line'. Vfws Boje and Niemann were both killed.

McCudden flew home, 'feeling very satisfied, having totally destroyed four enemy two-seaters that day'. This was the first time that an RFC pilot had destroyed four enemy machines in one day, and McCudden received many telegrams of congratulations. In the evening, the pilots went into Amiens for a celebratory dinner.

Snow and mist stopped all war flying on 24 December. On the 25th – the fourth Christmas Day of the war – low cloud and snow again cancelled all war flying. Instead, the date was celebrated in the time-honoured fashion. Dinner was a special event and the squadron band gave a concert, but McCudden commented 'we had a very quiet Christmas for Bowman, our star turn in the Mess, was in England on leave, having a thoroughly good time'.

McCudden took off alone on 28 December. It was a beautifully clear, crisp, winter's morning, with 20 degrees of frost and excellent visibility. He attacked a Rumpler coming from the direction of Bourlon Wood and shot its wings off, the wreckage falling in the British lines north of Vélu Wood. Uffz Munz and Ltn Rücker from *Fl Abt 7* were both killed. Fifteen minutes later McCudden saw another Rumpler, this time a machine from *Fl Abt 40*, crewed by Ltn Mittag and Uffz Güntert. It went down in flames, crashing near Flers, some 20 miles behind the British lines. McCudden's next victory was an LVG, flying at 16,000 ft over Havrincourt. Under his fire it went down in flames and broke up in mid-air. The crew, Ltn Bergmann and Flg Weinrich from *Fl Abt (A) 210*, were killed.

No 56 Sqn's famous band consisted of, in the back row, from left to right, H T Walters (bass), Flt Sgt H Smith (trombone), F H Pitt (cornet), Davies (violin) and W W A Mason (woodwind). In the second row, from left to right, are G H Rolls (Drums), J D Thomas (violin), P P Rossini (cello), unknown, W Milton (violin) and T Taylor. And in the front row seated, from left to right, are S R Pegg (snare drum), Sgt P E Gayer (violin and leader), unknown and E Cunningham (violin)

British anti-aircraft fire then pointed out another LVG just east of the lines. A long burst from McCudden's Lewis gun caused a small flame to appear within the fuselage, but this went out 'almost at once'. The enemy pilot dived away, steam and boiling water pouring from the wing-mounted radiator and the enemy observer leaning over the side of his cockpit in an attempt to escape the scalding fluid. McCudden had scant sympathy – 'I hope the water froze over him solid and gave him frostbite'. Balcombe Brown considered that this last LVG, although badly damaged, may not have crashed, and therefore refused to allow it as a victory unless confirmation was later received from AA batteries. McCudden was quite content, nevertheless, having shot down three two-seaters during the course of the morning.

The great ace was again in action the next morning too, this time leading his flight. The SE 5as attacked three two-seaters over Vaucelles Wood, with McCudden's opponent – an LVG from *Schusta* 10 – proving to be a wily customer. Fought down to ground level, the pilot switched off his engine and pretended that he was going to land behind the British lines. Switching on his engine again to clear a trench, he decided to make a run for it. Turning northeast, and flying only ten feet off the ground, he flew to Havrincourt, where he turned east for the safety of his own lines. McCudden could not allow this. He dived after the enemy machine and fired a short burst from a range of 100 yards. The LVG immediately spun away and crashed in the British lines near the remains of the LVG which McCudden had shot down on 23 November.

The ace circled the crash and watched the 'Tommies' helping the crew from the wreckage of their aeroplane. The pilot, Vfw Gerschel, was mortally wounded, but the gunner, Uffz Lehnert, survived to be taken prisoner.

Within 40 minutes of landing from this patrol, McCudden took off again, this time alone. His first combat was with an LVG over Lagnicourt, McCudden's fire hitting its radiator, but the enemy pilot dived away steeply to the east and escaped. Nearly two hours passed before McCudden found another LVG, this time over Gouzeaucourt at 15,000 ft. The enemy pilot circled to give his gunner the chance of a shot at the closing SE 5a. McCudden, however, waited, knowing that the pilot would eventually have to fly straight in order to escape over his own lines. When his opponent finally made his dash for safety, McCudden dived and fired until the LVG broke up, burst into flames and fell in the British lines northeast of Épéhy, killing both Ltns Dern and Müller from *Fl Abt* 33. McCudden returned, well pleased with the morning's work. 'I had a generous dinner, after which we listened to the gramophone for half-an-hour and life again seemed full of cheer'.

As in November, December had not been a good month for No 56 Sqn. Seventeen enemy aeroplanes and one balloon had been brought down, but four pilots had been lost – Maybery in action and three others in flying accidents. Fourteen of the enemy aeroplanes credited to the unit had fallen under the guns of McCudden. In fact, during December, McCudden *was* No 56 Sqn! The squadron's victory lists show his name for no less than ten consecutive victories. By the end of 1917 McCudden's personal score stood stood at 37, of which only three relied on his unsupported evidence. There can be little doubt that by the end of 1917 James McCudden was one of the most efficient destroyers of enemy aeroplanes yet seen in the skies above France.

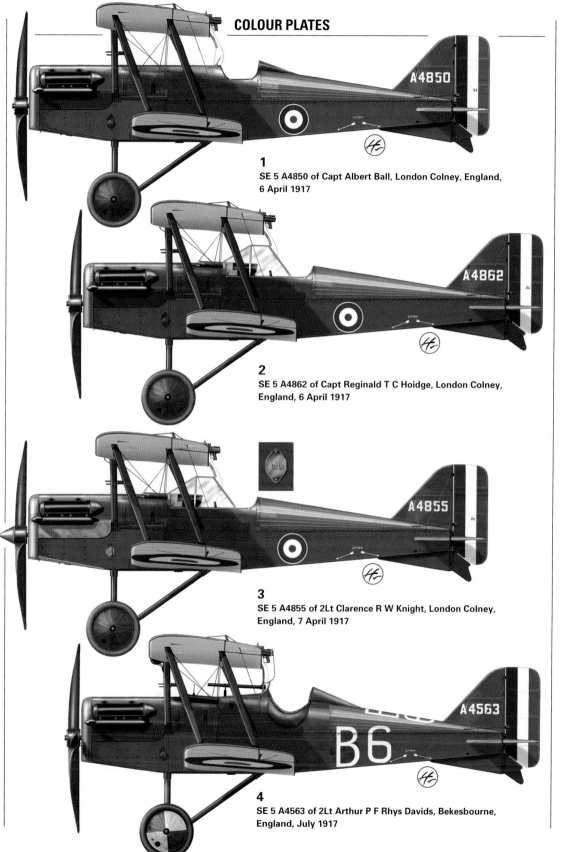

1
SE 5 A4850 of Capt Albert Ball, London Colney, England,
6 April 1917

2
SE 5 A4862 of Capt Reginald T C Hoidge, London Colney,
England, 6 April 1917

3
SE 5 A4855 of 2Lt Clarence R W Knight, London Colney,
England, 7 April 1917

4
SE 5 A4563 of 2Lt Arthur P F Rhys Davids, Bekesbourne,
England, July 1917

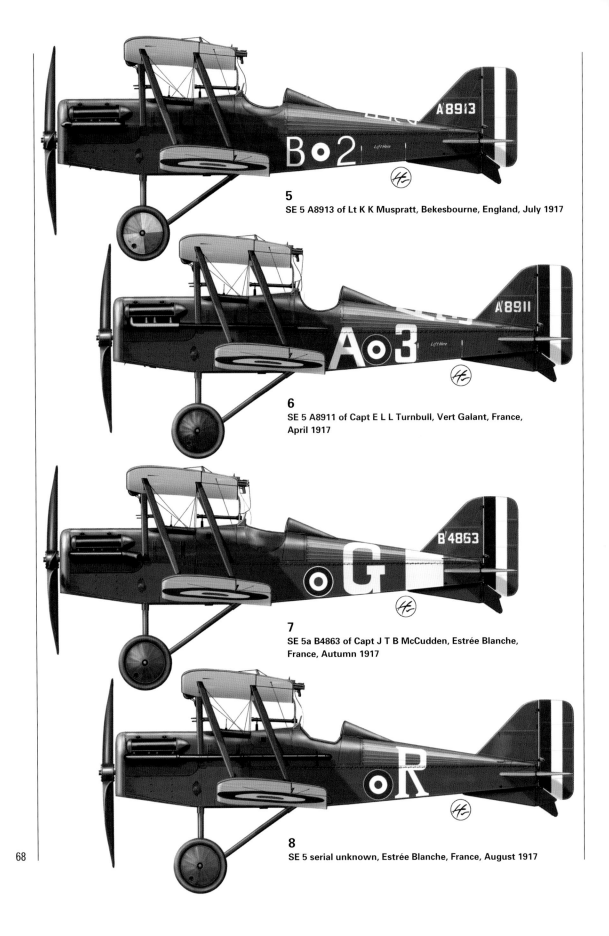

5
SE 5 A8913 of Lt K K Muspratt, Bekesbourne, England, July 1917

6
SE 5 A8911 of Capt E L L Turnbull, Vert Galant, France,
April 1917

7
SE 5a B4863 of Capt J T B McCudden, Estrée Blanche,
France, Autumn 1917

8
SE 5 serial unknown, Estrée Blanche, France, August 1917

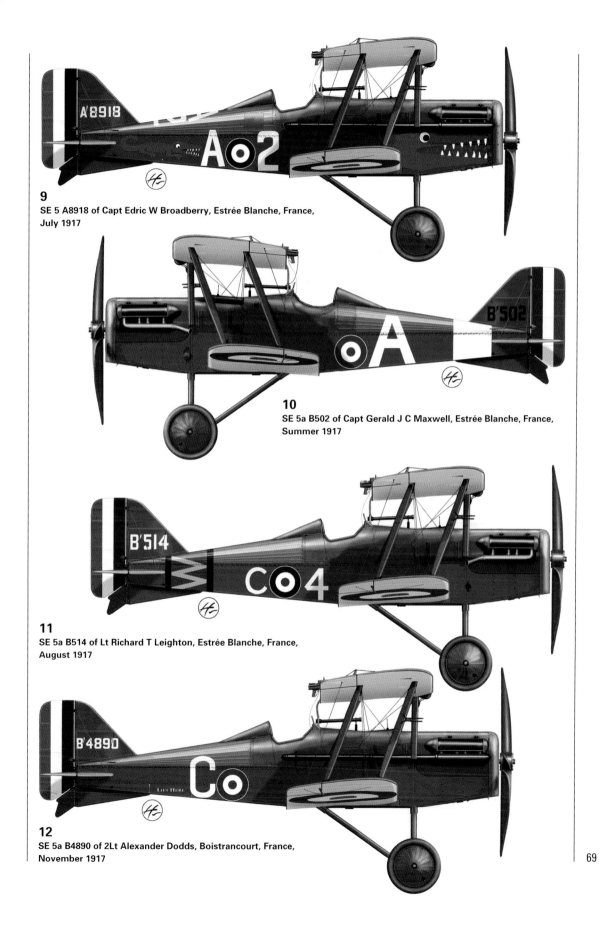

9
SE 5 A8918 of Capt Edric W Broadberry, Estrée Blanche, France,
July 1917

10
SE 5a B502 of Capt Gerald J C Maxwell, Estrée Blanche, France,
Summer 1917

11
SE 5a B514 of Lt Richard T Leighton, Estrée Blanche, France,
August 1917

12
SE 5a B4890 of 2Lt Alexander Dodds, Boistrancourt, France,
November 1917

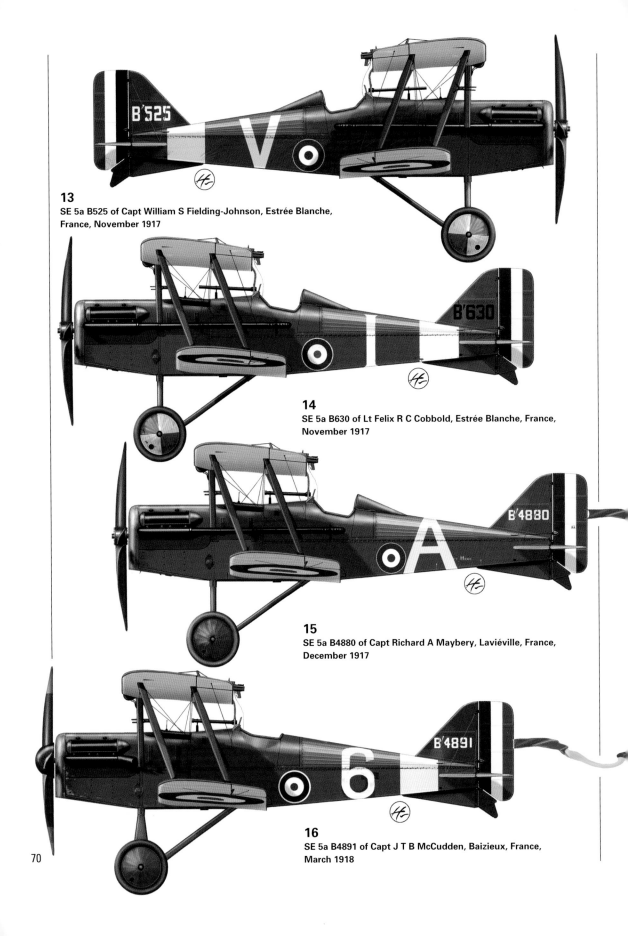

13
SE 5a B525 of Capt William S Fielding-Johnson, Estrée Blanche,
France, November 1917

14
SE 5a B630 of Lt Felix R C Cobbold, Estrée Blanche, France,
November 1917

15
SE 5a B4880 of Capt Richard A Maybery, Laviéville, France,
December 1917

16
SE 5a B4891 of Capt J T B McCudden, Baizieux, France,
March 1918

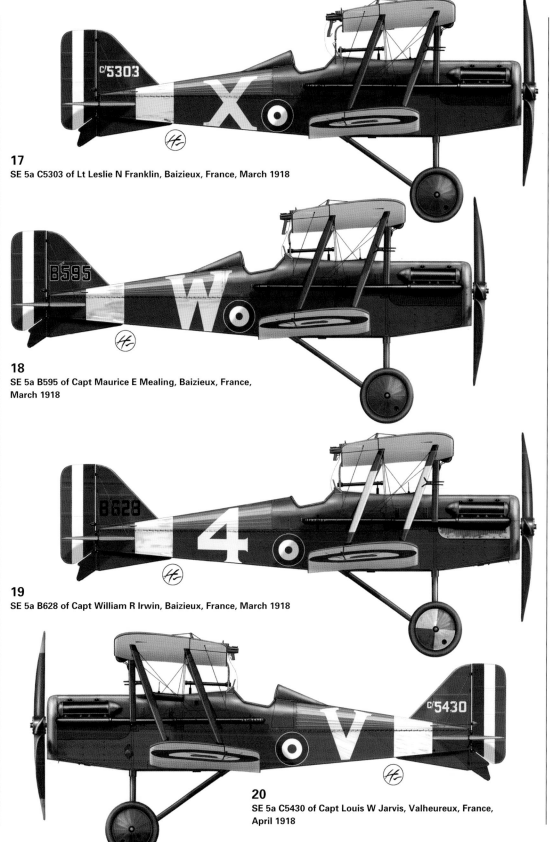

17
SE 5a C5303 of Lt Leslie N Franklin, Baizieux, France, March 1918

18
SE 5a B595 of Capt Maurice E Mealing, Baizieux, France,
March 1918

19
SE 5a B628 of Capt William R Irwin, Baizieux, France, March 1918

20
SE 5a C5430 of Capt Louis W Jarvis, Valheureux, France,
April 1918

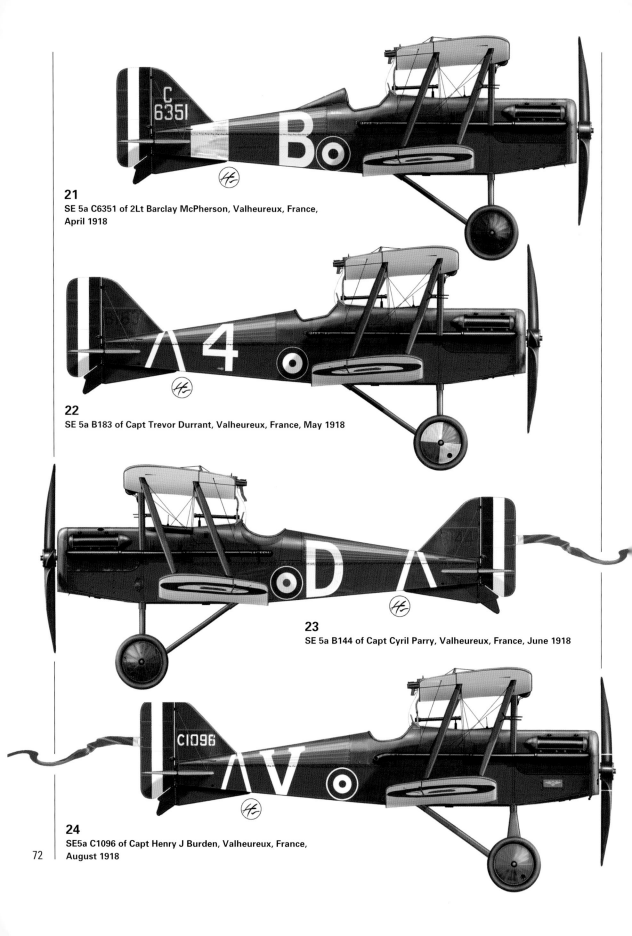

21
SE 5a C6351 of 2Lt Barclay McPherson, Valheureux, France,
April 1918

22
SE 5a B183 of Capt Trevor Durrant, Valheureux, France, May 1918

23
SE 5a B144 of Capt Cyril Parry, Valheureux, France, June 1918

24
SE5a C1096 of Capt Henry J Burden, Valheureux, France,
August 1918

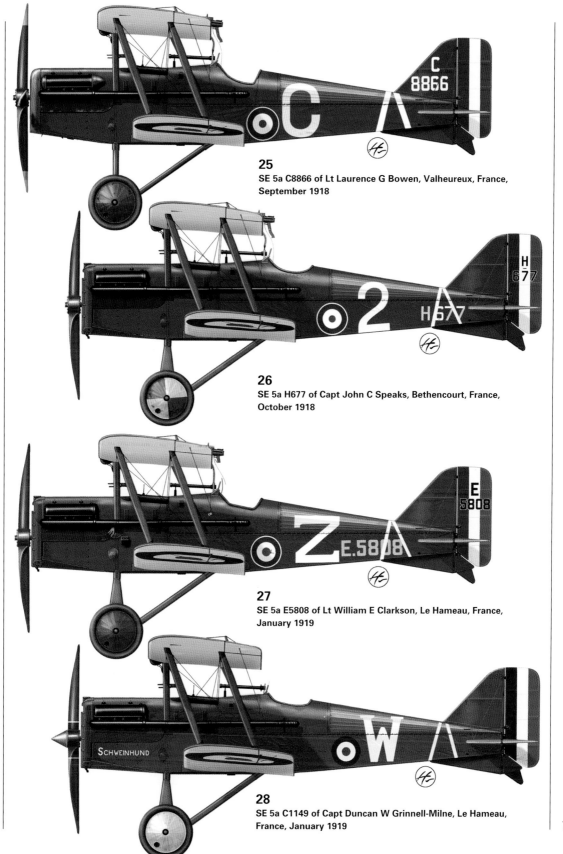

25
SE 5a C8866 of Lt Laurence G Bowen, Valheureux, France,
September 1918

26
SE 5a H677 of Capt John C Speaks, Bethencourt, France,
October 1918

27
SE 5a E5808 of Lt William E Clarkson, Le Hameau, France,
January 1919

28
SE 5a C1149 of Capt Duncan W Grinnell-Milne, Le Hameau,
France, January 1919

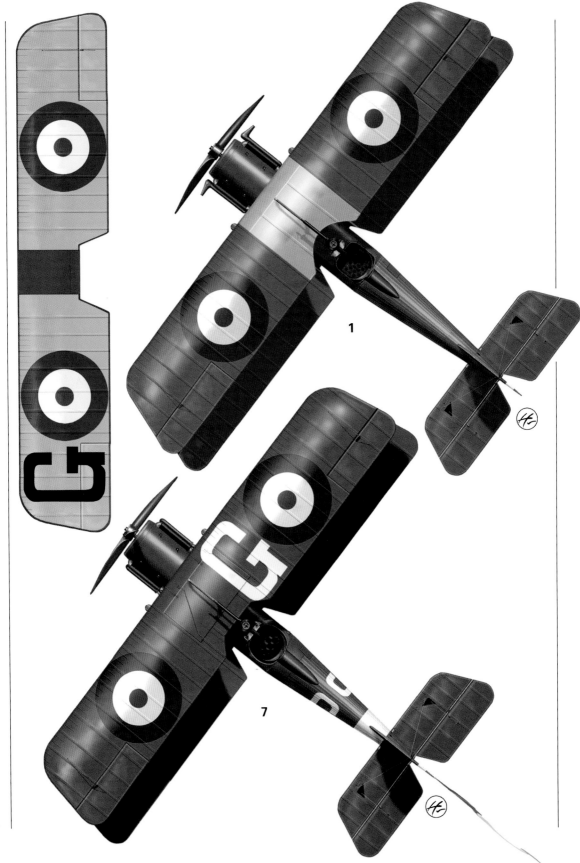

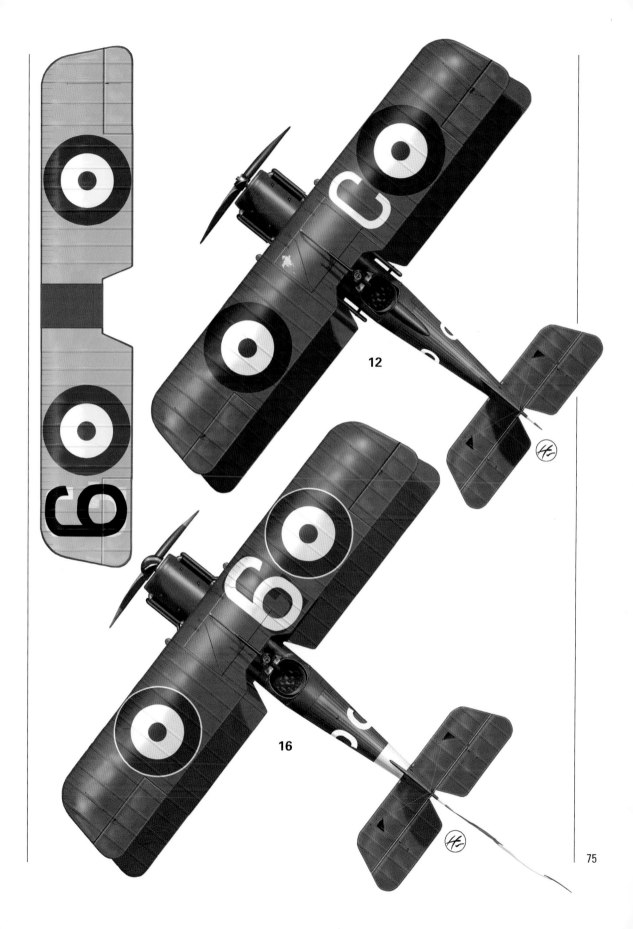

12

16

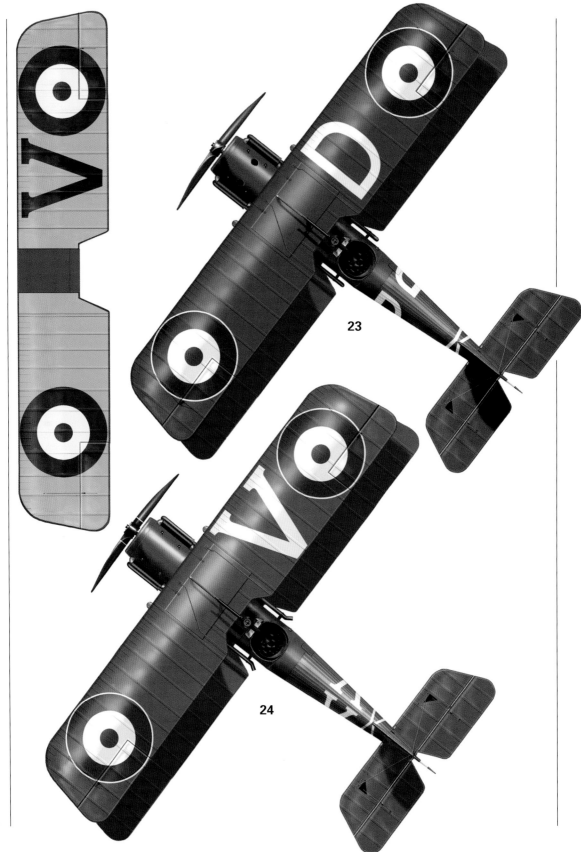

23

24

NEW YEAR AND NEW TACTICS

By the end of 1917 a new attitude towards the war in the air had evolved. The early concept that air fighting was a sport, albeit a dangerous one, had now largely disappeared. With the arrival at the fighter squadrons of officers who had already seen combat with other RFC units, or with frontline regiments on the ground, the last remaining vestiges of this sporting concept were finally dispelled. Like combat in the trenches, the air war was a hard and hazardous duty. It was now also recognised that it had to be skilfully and, above all, professionally fought. During 1917, brilliant flight commanders, of which McCudden was only one, began to emerge in the ranks of the RFC.

The new year started slowly for No 56 Sqn. McCudden, anxious to score the unit's 250th victory and his own flight's 100th, stayed up

The 'Unsung Heroes'. These men were some of the groundcrew assigned to A Flight in early 1918. In the back row, from left to right, are Fred Homer, Jock Allen, Cpl E Clements and Jack Charles. In the front row, from left to right, are Jack Cooper, Cpl E Ellison and Arthur Moody. Shortly after this photograph was taken, Cooper and Charles were promoted to corporal and Ellison to sergeant. In his evocative book *Wind in The Wires*, Grinnell-Milne was later to write of the squadron's groundcrews, 'Each man an expert in his own line, they had worked with a will. Upon their careful tuning of engines, their skilful adjustment of rigging wires and their accurate sighting of machine guns, many lives had long depended. The squadron's successes are theirs to share with the boldest of those pilots whose names still head the Honours board. The magic brilliance of letters "VC" twice repeated, shines on them as well – they helped to carve them'

for two hours in sub-zero temperatures, but failed to gain any decisive results from attacks on two-seaters. Alfred Blenkiron had better luck, shooting down an Albatros with a yellow fuselage and a black tail, which crashed between the railway line and the town of Bourlon. Blenkiron was confident that he could claim this as the squadron's 250th victory, but Balcombe Brown refused to allow it as a victory, pointing out that there was no independent confirmation.

The next day, a ground mist and clouds heavy with snow ruled out any war flying. Although conditions improved dramatically on 3 January and some actions were fought (one of which resulted in Robert Stewart being shot down just behind the German lines by Ltn Hanstein of *Jasta* 35 – Stewart became a PoW), none produced the 250th victory. Indeed, it was not until 9 January that McCudden had a decisive combat. He attacked a Hannover CL II over Bourlon at 1115 hrs, but his Aldis sight had frozen over and he was forced to aim using tracer rounds. The Hannover went down in a spiral, trailing water or petrol, but under control.

After an indecisive fight with an Albatros over Ribécourt, McCudden next attacked an LVG over Graincourt. It hit the ground in a flat glide down wind. Balcombe Brown allowed this as the squadron's 250th victory, reasoning that the crash would have been a bad one, given the steepness of the glide and the strong following wind. That evening, at a celebration dinner to mark the 250th victory, McCudden received a telegram from Gen J M Salmond, now GOC of the RFC, congratulating him on his being the first flight to have brought down 100 enemy aeroplanes.

Although the weather was fine on 13 January, visibility was 'indifferent' and there was a strong westerly wind. It was to be an unlucky day for three German two-seaters. McCudden took off alone at 0840 hrs. He first saw an LVG going north over Bellengise, and coming out of the sun he closed to within 50 yards before firing a short burst. The aircraft crashed east of Le Haucourt. McCudden next engaged a pair of DFWs, with a long burst from both guns sending one down in a vertical dive to hit the ground north of Vendhuile. McCudden then flew north until he spotted two LVGs flying over Éphéy. He attacked one from 200 yards, and firing 200 rounds of Vickers into it. The enemy machine went down in a vertical dive, its wings breaking off before it finally burst into flames and crashed in the British lines east of Lempire. After an indecisive engagement with a DFW, McCudden returned home. In just 20 minutes he had totally destroyed three enemy two-seaters.

During the inactivity of the previous few days, McCudden had instructed his mechanics to fit the spinner (which had first been painted brilliant red) from the LVG that he had shot down on 30 November to the nose of his SE 5a. Flying for the first time with the spinner on 13 January, and having shot down three two-seaters, McCudden was convinced it was bringing him luck. The first LVG he had destroyed was flown by Notler (rank unknown), with Ltn d R Max Pappenheimer as observer. Notler was uninjured, but Pappenheimer had been killed by McCudden's fire. The second victory (the DFW) crashed near Gouzeaucourt, killing crewmen Ltn Besser and Vfw Rautenberg from *Bogohl* 7. The third machine, another LVG also possibly from *Bogohl* 7, was the only one of the three to fall in the British lines, Ltn Rittermann of the *Bogohl* being reported as killed over Gonnelieu.

McCudden's SE 5a B4891 '6' in early 1918. This photograph shows the red spinner to advantage

After lunch on the 13th, McCudden left on a Special Duty to the 11th Wing. His technique of destroying enemy two-seaters, apparently with little effort, had come to the attention of Lt Col A J L Scott, CO of the wing, and he requested that McCudden visit the local fighter squadrons to lecture on his tactics.

On 20 January there was a great deal of fighting. Bowman attacked a pair of two-seaters over Bois de Cheneauz, his flight remaining above to protect him from five Fokker triplanes in the vicinity. Bowman failed to gain a result over the two-seaters, with bad gun trouble forcing him to break off the action. However, McCudden, who had returned from his lecture tour on 18 January, shot down an LVG over Bourlon Wood. The aircraft spiralled down smoking badly until its tailplane broke off at 5000 ft, the wreckage falling between Raillencourt and Cambrai. This LVG was possibly from *Fl Abt (A)* 202, crewed by Uffz Mosch and Ltn Bracksiek.

The squadron spent the morning of 21 January moving the short distance to Baizieux aerodrome. Although only a field away from Laviéville, the facilities were better and the landing area less tricky.

McCudden, Bowman and Blenkiron all took off on lone missions during the afternoon of 24 January. Bowman and Blenkiron aborted their flights because of the thick mist, but McCudden carried on. At 1355 hrs British anti-aircraft fire pointed out a DFW over Monchy-le-Preux. McCudden attacked the aircraft and sent it down out of control, alternately stalling and diving until it disappeared into the ground mist. This was McCudden's 43rd victory, and his sixth since the beginning of the year. He was the only pilot of the unit to have scored in over a month, but on 25 January the other pilots were to end their run of bad luck.

C Flight was first in action, with Bowman shooting the observer of an LVG. The latter fell back into his cockpit, his gun unattended, either dead or wounded. Blenkiron then attacked, forcing Bowman to zoom away.

Trevor Durrant enjoys a cigarette at Baizieux

Bowman went after another LVG, shooting it down into a quarry a mile northwest of Rumilly. Blenkiron had finished off the first LVG, Maurice Mealing had shot large pieces off another, sending it down out of control, and Douglas Woodman had shot down a fourth LVG from the formation of five.

New pilot Trevor Durrant, whom McCudden had described in fighting practise as being 'very good', shot down an LVG over Graincourt. After an indecisive skirmish with 'Greentail's' flight over Proville, McCudden then attacked a Rumpler over St Quentin. This aircraft, crewed by Ltns Schramm and Büscher of *Fl Abt (A)* 225, went down out of control over Urvillers. Schramm and Büscher were both wounded, the latter mortally.

On 26 January, Capt Eric Turnbull was posted to Home Establishment. He had served with the squadron two days short of eight months, which was an unusually long period occasioned by Maybery's death in December 1917 leaving the squadron short of experienced flight commanders. Len Baker recalled, 'He took great care of his patrols. I remember how he came round to each mechanic and rigger and shook hands when he was leaving. "Keep it going", he said. I won't mention all the replies he didn't hear. Anyway, he was a very nice chap'.

During the bad weather, McCudden had taken the opportunity to further modify his 'spinnered' SE 5a B4891. Chief amongst these modifications was the fitting of a set of high compression pistons. On the squadron's test bench, the re-pistoned engine gave considerably more revolutions per minute than the standard Hispano-Suiza motor, and McCudden had high hopes that it would enable him to catch and attack the Maybach-powered high-flying Rumpler C VIIs.

A combat on 28 January saw No 56 Sqn suffer its first casualty from enemy action since the 3rd of the month. In a fight with enemy scouts and two-seaters over Bourlon Wood, Lester Williams was shot down by the *Fl Abt (A)* 233 crew of Ltns Schuppau and Schandva. The RFC pilot was taken prisoner. Two days later McCudden shot down an Albatros scout, noting that 'Pieces of what looked like three-ply fell off the enemy aircraft, which turned to the left and went down in a vertical dive emitting smoke absolutely out of control'. This was the aircraft of Vfw Adam Barth of *Jasta* 10, who was killed. McCudden next turned his attentions to a Pfalz D III, which was sent down in a spiral dive over Fontaine.

The only squadron patrols made that day were flown by B and C Flights. In a fight with four 'V' Strutters over Wambaix, Canadian pilot Kenneth Junor shot down Oblt Bruno Justinus, who was the acting *Staffelführer* of *Jasta* 35b. The German pilot was thrown clear of his blazing aeroplane as it hit the ground, mercifully already dead from gunshot wounds. Ten minutes later, just to the north of Cambrai, C Flight was attacked by a pair of black-tailed Albatros 'V' Strutters that were quickly joined by five others. Bowman downed one of the black-tailed scouts, which crashed alongside a road.

A thick fog on 31 January effectively cancelled all flying.

PILOT TRAINING

During the first two months of 1918 No 56 Sqn had over a third of its pilots under training, with full advantage being taken of the bad weather to bring the unit up to full operational strength. Lts Parry, Stuart Maxwell, Morgan, Irwin, Macdonald, Hastings-Trew and Porter received instruction from the more experienced pilots on the squadron, and they also attended air gunnery courses at Berk-sur-Mere – a seaside resort in happier times.

There was no flying on the first day of February due to a thick mist covering the aerodrome, but at 1030 hrs on the 2nd McCudden took off alone, ostensibly on a 'weather test'. His combat report for the action that followed is as brief and matter of fact as the way in which he was now disposing of enemy two-seaters;

'At 1040 hrs I saw an LVG going northeast over Ruyaulcourt at 11,000 ft. I overtook the enemy aircraft, secured a firing position at 100 yards range and fired a long burst from both guns, after which the enemy aircraft went down vertically, then on its back, when the gunner fell out and the machine finally crashed in our lines one mile east of Velu at Sheet 57G J33. I returned at 1050 hrs to report weather.'

No further patrols were flown until the 16th. Weather conditions were generally bad, and the temperature was becoming progressively colder. Several horses were available for riding, and during this period of inactivity, Cyril Parry, who was an expert horseman, attempted to introduce McCudden to the joys of equestrian pursuits. The latter, who was perfectly at home with man-made methods of travel, was less so with the jogging motion of a horse, laughingly insisting that the animal was missing on one of its cylinders!

Parry was typical of the new type of officer, bringing a more professional outlook to the business of air fighting. He had joined the Royal Welch Fusiliers as a band boy in 1908, and by 1917 – now an NCO weapons instructor – had watched with increasing frustration each draft of men he had trained leave for France. Parry had applied for a transfer to the RFC and been accepted for pilot training, partly on the strength of his off-duty activity of exercising racehorses at nearby Newmarket. Making his first flight under instruction in October 1917, Parry had been posted to No 56 Sqn on 3 January. He was later to develop into a fine flight commander, basing his tactics on McCudden's teaching.

Eugene Ronald Macdonald, who was described by Cyril Parry as 'a quiet little chap, but when you looked round he was always there in the thick of it'

William Roy Irwin 'runs up' SE 5a B628 at Baizieux. The style of flight number and the B Flight markings of blue and white quartered wheel covers are well shown

8 February was a sad day for the unit as 'Beery' Bowman left to take command of No 41 Sqn – a position that he had been resisting for some time. On one of his periodic inspections, Gen Higgins stopped in front of Bowman and exclaimed 'What the devil are you doing here, Bowman? You should be commanding 41'. Bowman replied that he was happy with the squadron, and anyway, he did not know any of the aeroplanes at 41! Bowman had no compunction in talking to a general in such a manner. However, as he explained to the author, 'I was the one doing the blood and thunder stuff, and I thought I ought to have the choice of where I did it – and that was with 56'. After some argument, Higgins agreed that if 'Beery' would take up command of No 41 Sqn he could take his own SE 5a with him.

With Bowman's departure the squadron lost its last remaining link with its early days in France. He had served a remarkable nine months with the squadron as C Flight commander. Under his leadership, the flight had accounted for more than 80 enemy aeroplanes, 22 of these falling to Bowman's guns. But his worth lay even more in his personal example and leadership. Indeed, many pilots owed their later successes to Bowman's teachings.

On 16 February the squadron returned to active operations. McCudden and B Flight, with C Flight led by its new commander, William Fielding-Johnson, took off at 0935 hrs. Their duty was to escort a reconnaissance formation of Bristol Fighters, but while circling over Caudry waiting for the Bristols to arrive, McCudden saw a Rumpler climbing for height over the town. Never one to let an opportunity pass, he attacked. The Rumpler went down in a vertical dive, all four wings breaking off. The fuselage fell

The wreckage of LVG C V 9775/17 from *Boghol* 7, crewed by Ltns Werner von Kuczowski and Erich Szafranek, who were both killed. It was shot down by McCudden on 2 February 1918 for his 47th victory

William Spurrett Fielding-Johnson in SE 5a B37 'U' in March 1918

south of the town, the wings following more slowly, spreading over a wide area of countryside. Uffz Hänicke and Ltn Düsterdieck of *Fl Abt (A)* 269 were both killed.

Ten minutes later McCudden despatched a DFW from *Fl Abt (A)* 202, crewed by Ltn Karlowa and Uffz Föhlich. The aircraft went down in flames before finally breaking up, the wreckage falling near Le Catelet. As he watched the two-seater going down, McCudden was startled to hear bullets hitting his SE 5a. Upon looking up he saw 'Greentail' above him. The German flight commander had tried a long range snipe, hitting McCudden's machine in several places and putting an elevator out of action. Seeing that he had been observed, 'Greentail' made off.

McCudden's windscreen and Aldis gunsight were by now covered with ice due to a radiator leak, but these troubles, and the inoperative elevator, did not prevent him shooting down a Rumpler as he crossed the lines over Havrincourt. The enemy machine went down in a steep dive, smoke pouring from it. Fielding-Johnson later saw the aircraft go into a right hand spiral dive, and he confirmed the victory. McCudden was delighted by this, as the Rumpler was his 50th success, making him the first British pilot to achieve the half-century. However, Balcombe Brown refused to allow the aircraft as a victory on Fielding-Johnson's confirmation alone.

McCudden was extremely angry at this, and he took off again 15 minutes later, determined to prove his point. By the time the ace sighted a possible victim, his anger had subsided and he stalked a Rumpler from *Schusta* 29, crewed by Vfw Zeuch and Gefr Lechleiter, with his usual care. A short burst sent the aircraft down, and it finally broke up, the wreckage falling in the British lines near Lagnicourt. Both the crew were killed. Balcombe Brown endorsed McCudden's combat report with 'This is the 50th enemy machine accounted for by Capt McCudden'. That same evening an AA battery rang No 56 Sqn to confirm the disputed victory of the first Rumpler.

83

McCudden now knew that he was coming to the end of his tour with the squadron. Anxious to increase his score before he was posted, he again took off alone on the morning of 17 February. Over Guemappe, he attacked a DFW that was being escorted by a Hannover C type. The latter hurriedly made off, leaving the DFW to its fate. McCudden fired a burst from both guns and the enemy machine side-slipped down into the ground mist. Its demise was later confirmed by AA batteries. McCudden then returned to Baizieux to have a malfunctioning Vickers gun repaired.

With the weapon fixed, he took off for the frontlines once again, and after an hour saw a Rumpler at 17,000 ft over Bourlon Wood. McCudden carefully stalked the two-seater for 45 minutes, struggling to get up to its height of 21,000 ft. Finally, his mission finished, the enemy pilot dived for home. This was McCudden's chance, but to his frustration the belt of his Vickers gun had broken and the Lewis gun was frozen. The Rumpler crew made good their escape.

Kenneth Junor also took off alone at 1025 hrs. Over Bourlon Wood, he was attacked from behind by an Albatros, but the enemy pilot missed and continued down. Junor dived after the German machine and shot it down in flames. This 'Albatros' was in fact a two-seat Hannover CL II from *Fl Abt (A)* 263, which lost Ltn Jablosnki and Vfw Klauke over Bourlon. In the afternoon, Capt Fielding-Johnson shot down an Albatros out of control, the fighter last being seen falling at 3000 ft. However, Balcombe Brown refused to allow this as a victory. During the fight, Mealing had shot down another of the enemy scouts, watching it crash near Brancourt-le-Grand. This was confirmed by Capt Jarvis.

The first patrol on 18 February resulted in a great deal of satisfaction for the squadron. B Flight attacked a formation of four Albatros scouts over

Leslie N Franklin in SE 5a C5303 'X'. The man standing at the left is unknown, but by the nose is rigger Flt Sgt C Gibson

Vitry-en-Artois, with McCudden's fire hitting the leader's Albatros, which burst into flames. Its pilot was seen to fall from his blazing machine. McCudden then shot down a blue-tailed Albatros, which crashed between Beaumont and Quiery-le-Motte, north of Vitry-en-Artois.

The ace was convinced that the Albatros he had downed in flames was 'Greentail', as the scout had a large white chevron on the top wing and the letter 'K' on the fuselage. This victory provoked a sense of satisfaction within No 56 Sqn, whose pilots believed that Maybery had been shot down by 'Greentail'. However, the latter was almost certainly a pilot of *Jasta* 5, and these two Albatros were from *Jasta* 35b. The first machine was flown by Uffz Julius Kaiser, who was killed, while the second scout, with the blue tail, was flown by Uffz Joachim von Stein. Although wounded in the left shoulder, neck and mouth, Stein managed to crash-land his badly damaged Albatros.

The next day McCudden had two indecisive engagements with Hannovers. However, during a later patrol by C Flight, Fielding-Johnson sent a two-seater out of control southwest of Rumaucourt. One of four machines encountered by the flight, its demise was later confirmed by AA batteries. Louis Jarvis and Frank Billinge also despatched a second machine in a wide right hand spiral, having either killed or wounded the observer.

On 21 February, after leading his flight on a patrol during which he drove an LVG back across its own lines, McCudden took off alone after

C Flight at Baizieux. These pilots are, from left to right, M E Mealing, W S Fielding-Johnson (flight commander), H J Walkerdine, L W Jarvis, L N Franklin and A L Garrett

William Louis Jarvis, seen here in SE 5a C5430 V, was C Flight commander from 29 April to 24 May 1918

lunch. Finding a DFW over Achville, McCudden attacked it, but he only had time for six shots before the enemy pilot dived for the ground. Zooming away from the two-seater, he looked back to see the DFW going down in flames. The aircraft crashed on the railway line just south of Méricourt, the aircraft's demise being confirmed by three AA batteries of the 1st Army.

No 56 Sqn did very little flying over the next four days due to the onset of poor weather. On the 25th, McCudden, nursing a bad cold, was visited by Lt Col Patrick Playfair, OC No 13 Wing, who told him that he was to be posted home in the near future. He also ordered him to refrain from flying any further missions during the remainder of his time with the squadron. McCudden was extremely annoyed at these orders, as he was anxious to add to his score and rival that of Manfred von Richthofen, whose last victory – his 63rd – had been claimed as long ago as 30 November 1917.

Despite Playfair's ruling, McCudden was determined to fly as much as possible before his posting home, and he was therefore delighted when the weather improved on the morning of 26 February. Although still suffering from a sore throat and feeling extremely ill, McCudden took off alone at 0955 hrs and found an LVG over Gonnelieu. The enemy pilot manoeuvred his machine 'like a fighter' and finally dived away to the east. This aircraft was marked with a large '6' on the top wing in an identical manner to McCudden's SE 5a. After the action McCudden was immediately attacked by three Albatros scouts, but these were driven off by a formation of SE 5as from No 84 Sqn. McCudden then flew north and attacked a pair of Hannovers, but these were both flown by experienced crews who cooperated well.

Leaving these dangerous opponents, McCudden flew to Douai and attacked a Rumpler directly over the town. Opening fire at 200 yards, he continued firing until the Rumpler burst into flames and broke up, the pieces falling east of Oppy. McCudden then turned south and attacked a DFW, and its escorting Hannover, over Chérisy. The DFW dived away, but the Hannover stayed to fight. McCudden, feeling light-headed and feverish, was determined to down his opponent;

'I had never destroyed one before, so I said to myself "I'm going to shoot down that Hannover or be shot down in the attempt". I secured my firing position, and placing my sight on the Hannover's fuselage, I fired both guns until the two-seater fell to pieces.'

This aircraft was to be McCudden's 57th, and last, victory. He later attacked two Rumplers, firing at one until he expended all his ammunition. Pieces fell off the enemy machine, but it escaped over its own lines. Reaction now set in to McCudden's exertions, and he felt extremely ill. The ace managed to return home, however, and after a hot drink and a rest he felt better.

On reflection, McCudden believed that the LVG marked with the number '6' had possibly been a decoy sent up by the Germans in an attempt to destroy the pilot of the SE 5a marked with a '6' on the wings that had caused such havoc amongst the two-seaters units in previous months.

A patrol by A Flight later that same day claimed an LVG, after which it attacked a formation of Albatros scouts over Sans-les-Marquion, diving at them from out of the sun. Following these combats, the LVG was credited to Barclay McPherson and an Albatros out of control to Ken Junor. This patrol was the last to be flown by the squadron in February. The month had been a good one for the squadron, for it had lost no pilots in action. Despite the bad weather, the unit had accounted for 17 enemy aeroplanes. Once again McCudden had been the most successful pilot by some considerable margin, downing 11 of them.

Capt McCudden and his B Flight at Baizieux in late February 1918. Only the following individuals have been identified to date – back row, from left to right, Cpl Ernest Etherington (sixth from left), and front row, from left to right, Cpl E A Downing (seated, extreme left), Cpl Albert Card, who was McCudden's engine mechanic (seated, second from left), Technical Sgt Maj Peter J Clark (third from left), McCudden (fourth from left), Sgt E Vousden (fourth from right), V L Reeves (third from right), Cpl Tom Rogers (engine mechanic, second from right) and G 'Dobby' Dobriskey (extreme right)

KAISERSCHLACHT

By the beginning of March, No 56 Sqn had lost three experienced flight commanders in a little over six weeks. Capt Fielding-Johnson, commanding C Flight, was now the only pilot with experience. Billinge, commanding A Flight, had flown over 200 hours as an observer but suffered from airsickness above 12,000 ft and was eventually posted out of the unit in April. The departure of McCudden back to the UK on 5 March for service with the Home Establishment further exacerbated the problem, but his replacement was a particularly happy solution.

Cyril Crowe, who had been the original B Flight commander in April 1917, was anxious to return to France, even offering to be demoted a rank – he was now a major – in order to do so, and he arrived as McCudden's replacement on 3 March. The unit was pleased to have the nine-victory ace back, for Crowe was exceedingly popular, and his personality was a great boost to morale.

On 2 March a farewell dinner was held for James McCudden. A table had been booked at Gobelins, the famous restaurant in Amiens, and more then 50 officers attended. It was a splendid occasion, and McCudden admitted in his autobiography, *Five Years in the Royal Flying Corps*, that later, in the privacy of his bunk, he cried at the thought of leaving the squadron. To McCudden, as with many young pilots, the camaraderie of a squadron on active service – despite the dangers – was almost that of a family.

It is impossible to exaggerate the worth and value of McCudden to No 56 Sqn. During his eight months as commander of B Flight, the latter had gained 77 victories, with McCudden's share of the total being 52. This impressive score had been achieved for the loss of only four pilots – an indication of McCudden's excellence as a patrol leader and the care he took of his pilots. Few flight commanders in the RFC at that time looked after their less experienced pilots anywhere near as well as McCudden. However, the ace's strategy had been simple – the greatest number of victories for the lowest number of casualties. The apparent ease with which McCudden destroyed enemy two-seaters is also deceptive, giving the impression that these were easy opponents. This is far from the truth, as these enemy two-seaters were fast, well armed and flown by well-trained and experienced crews.

The first combat of the new month was fought on 6 March, when two Hannovers were seen over Cambrai with a pair of Albatros scouts – one with a black and white striped tail – as escorts. Billinge, attacking one of the two-seaters, was in turn targeted by an Albatros and a general melée began. 'The enemy aircraft was fighting and flying extraordinarily well', Billinge later recalled. Only Leslie Franklin scored during the confused fighting, shooting at an Albatros which half stalled and then spun a number of times, before turning over onto its back and going down.

The next victory came on 8 March. Maurice Mealing shot down a two-seater over Villers-Outréaux and another over Homblières for his fifth and sixth victories. Three days later No 56 Sqn suffered its first combat casualty since the end of January. In a fight with Fokker triplanes

William Spurrett Fielding-Johnson was serving as an observer in No 3 Sqn in 1915 when this photograph was taken. He joined No 56 Sqn in October 1917, where he scored six victories and added a Bar to the MC that he had won earlier in the conflict. In World War 2 Fielding-Johnson served as an air gunner and was awarded a DFC

A group of pilots sit together at Baizieux in February/March 1918. They are, from left to right, Douglas Woodman, Eugene R Macdonald, Barclay McPherson, Henry J Burden and Cyril Parry. Only Douglas Woodman of this group failed to survive the war, being killed on 11 March 1918. McPherson was shot down and taken prisoner on 1 April – the day the RAF was formed

of *Jasta* 11, Lt Douglas Woodman was shot down and killed by future ace Vfw Edgar Scholtz for his second victory.

On 12 March Mealing attacked a two-seater over Ribecourt and shot it down to crash in the British lines near the town. Its pilot, Ltn Heinemann of *Fl Abt (A)* 259, was killed and the observer taken prisoner.

A great deal of action was fought three days later when C Flight, led by Fielding-Johnson, engaged ten yellow and orange Albatros scouts just north of Bourlon Wood. Mealing sent one of the enemy scouts down in a 'terrific spin', and although Fielding-Johnson fired at another that spun down past him, the fighting was so fierce that he could not watch it any further. Franklin saw an Albatros in flames, which was awarded to Fielding-Johnson, and Burden watched another spin into the ground, which was awarded to Mealing. These enemy scouts were possibly from *Jasta* 58, which lost Vfw August Wagner killed in action over Bourlon Wood. After this engagement, Mealing and Fielding-Johnson shared a Hannover, possibly from *Fl Abt (A)* 293, crewed by Uffz Seim and Ltn Sommer, both of whom were killed.

16 March again saw C Flight in the thick of the action, attacking four Albatros scouts. All of the latter machines were sent spinning down, but only two were seen to definitely pull out. Jarvis and Walkerdine were each awarded a victory. The flight then took on a pair of Hannover CL IIs north of Bourlon Wood. As Kenneth Knaggs was diving to attack these the wings of his SE 5a folded up and the machine fell apart. His demise was credited to Vfw Steinemeyer and Ltn Tittmann of *Fl Abt (A)* 240.

On the morning of 18 March, A and C Flights took off at 0620 hrs with orders to escort the Camels of No 3 Sqn that were to ground strafe in the vicinity of Bullecourt. The latter were attacked by ten enemy scouts – Albatros and Pfalz – and a general fight began. Walkerdine destroyed a Pfalz, which crashed northeast of Marquion, and sent another down in a

Sgt Walter Keen (left) and Cpl Jim Heggie (a C Flight engine mechanic) stand by SE 5a B8266 with H J 'Jackie' Walkerdine in the cockpit

Frank Billinge was A Flight commander from 15 February 1918 to 22 April 1918. He had previously served as an observer with No 20 Sqn, when this photograph was taken. After training as a pilot, Billinge served with No 32 Sqn, flying DH 2s, where he added two victories to the one he was awarded while with No 20 Sqn. During his time with No 56 Sqn Billinge added another two victories, taking his final tally to five

spin west of the town. Fielding-Johnson also attacked a Pfalz, which crashed near Buissy, and another that spun into the ground near the Bois de Cocret. He then set his sights on an Albatros, which went down steeply with smoke trailing from its fuselage. Looking down, Fielding-Johnson could see four crashed Pfalz and one other machine which he watched land near Bois de Cocret. Later in the morning, Crowe killed or wounded the observer in a two-seater, before shooting down another, which crashed near the lake north of Ecourt St Quentin.

Low clouds and rain made flying impossible on 19 and 20 March, but the German offensive on the 21st saw a return to action for No 56 Sqn. That day, the German Army launched Operation *Michael*, which targeted the British Third and Fifth Armies. Nearly 6000 guns opened fire on a 40-mile front between the Rivers Sensée and Oise. At Baizieux, No 56 Sqn was in the middle of the area under attack. At 0930 hrs, when German storm troopers began their advance, the battlefield was shrouded in a thick fog – ideal conditions for the enemy's shock troops, but not for the RFC units charged with defending their brethren who were being overwhelmed in the trenches.

Despite the weather conditions, two flights took off at 1250 hrs and saw a great deal of fighting. Trevor Durrant shot at a 'V' Strutter, which went down inverted, and Henry Burden attacked another. This disappeared into the ground mist, but a few seconds later there was a burst of flame and a column of black smoke. Mealing heard machine gun fire directly above him, and when he looked up he saw a triplane attacking an SE 5a, its wheels only just above his centre section! 'I pulled down my Lewis and fired half a drum of ammunition right into his fuselage, just below the pilot's seat'. The enemy triplane went down out of control.

The next day, A Flight saw the most fighting. In the afternoon, aided by 12 Camels from No 70 Sqn, it attacked a formation of 20 enemy machines – Fokker Dr Is, Albatros and Halberstadt CL IIs – north of Flesquières. Billinge claimed an Albatros out of control and Porter a triplane. Two of the 'V' Strutters forced Junor down to 2000 ft, but he outmanoeuvred one and shot it down to crash on the edge of Havrincourt Wood.

The morning of 23 March was misty, but the British position on the ground was now so desperate that flying was essential. The first patrol found the enemy aerodromes covered by thick fog. With no German aerial activity, Mealing and Walkerdine shot down a balloon. Turning away from the balloon, Mealing spotted a two-seater at low-level over Noreuil. The enemy pilot saw the SE 5as coming, turned sharply right, stalled and crashed into a trench between Lagnicourt and Noreuil before the RFC pilots had fired a single shot. The flight then flew to Queant railway station and strafed troops detraining with their equipment.

Two more flights took off at noon. Mealing's account of the patrol gives a vivid account of events that were typical of the actions during March;

'Crossed lines at 1230 hrs at 8000 ft over Equancourt. Ten Camels were at 9000 ft and A Flight was at 11,000 ft. Then saw about seven Camels crossing very low by Bapaume-Cambrai road, so went above them and went after ten enemy scouts to the east of the Camels. Enemy aircraft went east hard. Watched Camels back to the lines as more enemy aircraft were above us. Then climbed hard to reach two formations of enemy aircraft, but they climbed too. Triplanes remained above us and would not attack and Albatros scouts were too far east, although we got to their level.'

During the afternoon of the 23rd, ground strafing attacks were carried out on enemy troops on the Vaulx-Vrancourt-to-Lagnicourt road.

The weather was fine on 24 March. On the ground, the situation was desperate, with the Flesquières Salient being evacuated as the British Army pulled back in full retreat. It was essential that as many patrols as possible were flown in an effort to stall the enemy's advance. In an intense fight in the afternoon, Junor's SE 5a was badly damaged, forcing him to land near Bray in a machine that he described as 'shot to pieces'. William Porter was shot down and killed by a pilot from *Jasta* 34 in the same engagement. Also a participant in this melee, Eugene Macdonald found himself alone, but then saw a Pfalz close by. 'I got in the first burst at close range and he went down completely out of control'. Mealing shot down another of the Pfalz, which was flown by the leader of the enemy formation – it crashed east of Tincourt. This was possibly Oblt Ludwig Cordes of *Jasta* 16, who was killed on this date.

The remainder of the day was taken up with ground strafing operations along the whole of the front, which resulted in No 56 Sqn suffering yet another casualty. After ground strafing, 14-victory ace Maurice Mealing had last been seen attacking a pair of two-seaters over Le Transloy. David Galley later reported than he had seen an SE 5a on the ground behind enemy lines, and that the pilot, who he was sure was Mealing, waved at him as he flew overhead. However, the Germans later dropped a note to say that Mealing was dead. He was claimed by a two-seater crew from *Fl Abt (A)* 245, but there is reason to suppose that he had been killed by the German troops he had previously been attacking.

All pilots in No 56 Sqn made a great number of strafing attacks on the advancing German infantry during this period, but David Galley was particularly aggressive. Indeed, two of the patrols that he flew on 24 March earned him the MC, while Walkerdine, Junor, Mealing and Fielding-Johnson also received this gallantry medal for their exploits during the month of March.

Eight-victory ace Ken Junor poses with his SE 5a *BUBBLY KID II*.

Maurice Edward Mealing was killed in action on 24 March 1918. He had claimed 14 victories prior to his death

Officers from No 56 Sqn are presented to His Majesty King George V on the afternoon of 29 March 1918. His Majesty took the opportunity to tell the unit that he had approved the award of a Victoria Cross to James McCudden. These men are, from left to right, the Duke of Connaught, Balcombe Brown, the King, Parry, Tarbutt, Macdonald and Junor. The offficers obscured by the King are not named

The squadrons of the Fifth Army had been forced to evacuate their aerodromes on the first day of the offensive, and by the evening of 24 March it was evident that Baizieux itself was directly threatened by the storm troops of Gen von Below's 17th Army. Balcombe Brown flew to view an aerodrome at Valheureux and the squadron moved there the following day.

The next aerial success for No 56 Sqn came on 27 March. Jarvis and Walkerdine fired at an Albatros, which crashed in a ploughed field. Burden sent another down in a series of spins, but the enemy pilot regained control and attempted a down-wind landing, hitting the middle of a road and bouncing into the adjoining field. In an evening patrol, fighting with seven Fokker triplanes from *Jasta* 'Boelcke', Stewart Maxwell was shot down in flames by future six-victory ace Ltn Hermann Vallendor. Maxwell's great friend and fellow Scot Eugene Macdonald had the unhappy task of writing to Maxwell's parents to tell them of the death of their son.

Although the bad weather returned the next day, escort patrols were still flown for the ground-strafing Camels of No 3 Sqn. On 29 March – a day of high winds and intermittent rain – the squadron was inspected by King George V, who informed them unofficially that he had approved the award of the Victoria Cross to Capt McCudden for his work with the squadron. No flying was possible on 30 March, and on the last day of the month a patrol was flown but no enemy aeroplanes were seen.

March had been a bad month for the squadron, which had had five pilots killed in action – the highest number of casualties since the previous October.

The morning of 1 April (the birthday of the Royal Air Force) was fine. The first patrol of the day surprised ten Fokker triplanes with black and white tails over Guillemont, but only Junor managed to score, the others spinning away from the attack. By noon both Barclay McPherson and Frank Beaumont had been shot down and taken prisoner after duelling with German aces. McPherson had become the 11th victim of Hptm Wilhelm Reinhard of *Jasta* 6, while Beaumont was victory number 16 for Vfw Otto Könnecke of *Jasta* 5.

A combination of bad weather and a paucity of enemy aircraft meant that No 56 Sqn had to wait until 6 April to avenge these losses. Durrant had become separated from his formation in the cloudy conditions when he was attacked by five Fokker triplanes. Thanks to the SE 5a's superior speed, Durrant avoided these fighters and found a pair of two-seaters to engage near Lamotte instead, sending one down to crash – he spotted its tail sticking up out of the wreckage. This was possibly a machine from *Schutzstaffel* 31b.

On 11 April, Junor shot down an Albatros that boasted 'a white circle around small black crosses on top of its wings', the scout crashing just west of Aveluy. Shortly after this success, a formation of six Albatros scouts with black and white tailplanes, led by an all-red Fokker triplane, was spotted manoeuvring to attack the flight. The SE 5as outclimbed them, however, and launched an attack of their own west of Pozières. Durrant engaged one Albatros and shot it down in flames over Ovillers, killing Vfw Stemmeir of *Jasta* 76b. Jarvis went after a Pfalz, which had joined in the fight, and it crashed near Bécourt. This machine, which had its national markings in white circles on its upper wings, was possibly from *Jasta* 35b. Its pilot, Ltn d R Beyschlag, force-landed but was unhurt, and his Pfalz was later destroyed by British artillery.

The all-red triplane had stayed above the action, its pilot possibly hoping to pick off a straggler, but Ken Junor climbed above the mêlée and

Harold John 'Jackie' Walkerdine was wounded in action 11 April 1918. Although seriously injured in a flying accident in October 1918, he survived the war and passed away on 18 June 1966, the flying helmet that he had been wearing on 11 April 1918 being cremated with him. Throughout his life Walkerdine proudly wore two mementos of his days in the RFC – an artificial kneecap and his RFC tie

Relaxing in the orchard at Valheureux are, from left to right, Durrant, Garrett, Burden, Jarvis and Galley

Kenneth William Junor was killed in action on 23 April 1918. Like Durrant, he perished on the same day that he was promoted to command A Flight

'chased it off'. The popular 'Jackie' Walkerdine had attacked an Albatros head on, and fire from the latter machine hit the SE 5a. Two bullets shattered Walkerdine's windscreen and grazed his head. He quickly landed and was taken to hospital. Balcombe Brown's telegram to Walkerdine's parents was hardly reassuring – 'Your son wounded in head in action. Nothing dangerous, do not worry'!

Despite 12 April being a fine day, activity was only 'slight'. The weather changed the following day, and there was no war flying until the 20th. During this impromptu period of rest, Henry Burden wrote a long letter to Walkerdine, recovering in hospital, finishing with some good advice. 'Take all the time you need, and for goodness sake son don't start flying again until you have to. And don't take any flannel money. Best wishes old boy, and do drop a line soon to old Harrie'.

On 15 April, Brigadier Higgins wrote to Balcombe Brown asking that some pilots be detailed to shoot down German reconnaissance machines 'as McCudden used to do'. Balcombe Brown chose Fielding-Johnson, Billinge, Junor, Galley and Durrant for this task. Accordingly, Junor took off alone on the morning of the 20th and shot down a Rumpler, its wings breaking off and the fuselage bursting into flames, before finally crashing near Puisieux. Both crewmen, Ltn d R Trancre and Offz Stv Hoffman of *Fl Abt (A)* 263, were killed.

During the next few days several combats were fought with enemy formations that comprised both Albatros scouts and Fokker triplanes, and in one such fight, on 23 April, Capt Ken Junor was shot down and killed by future ace Ltn Egon Koepsch of *Jasta* 4. Although the War Diary of *Jagdgeschwader* 1 gives Koepsch's victory as 0655 hrs, Junor's was the only SE 5 lost that day, and with exception of this 12-hour difference (allowing for the one hour time differential in German time) all the facts – place and time – fit for Junor's loss. It therefore seems probable that the War Diary of JG1 was in error in giving the time as am instead of pm. The squadron could ill afford the loss of Junor, who, with eight victories to his name, had shown great potential as a future flight commander.

There was no flying for the remainder of the month as weather conditions deteriorated once again. On 24 April Capt Frank Billinge came to the end of his tour and was posted home, followed on 29 April by Fielding-Johnson. With the loss of Billinge and Fielding-Johnson, plus Junor's death, the squadron was again short of experienced flight commanders. Capt Edward Dawson 'Spider' Atkinson, a pilot of considerable experience who was on temporary attachment to the squadron on a refresher course, was given acting command of a flight, and Jarvis, returning from leave on 29 April, took over C Flight.

April had been an unproductive month for No 56 Sqn, with only seven victories claimed (five destroyed and two out of control) for the loss of four pilots – one killed, one wounded and two taken prisoner. May was to be little better.

VALHEUREUX – THE HAPPY VALLEY

No 56 Sqn was now settled in at Valheureux, more properly known as Le Valheureux – 'the Happy Valley' – which was to be its base for nearly seven months. Eugene Macdonald described the Mess;

'Our dining and annex marquees would have appeared fantastic to anyone from the frontline trenches. These marquees had an interior lining of cream coloured material, which gave a pleasant appearance. Electric lighting was from a workshop lorry. Our tables always looked beautiful – clean white tablecloths, gleaming cutlery, and nearly always flowers. Food was excellent, service perfect. We sent a Crossley tender down to Boulogne every second

The Mess at Valheureux – 'a wooden building, rather like a cricket pavilion'

day for fish. Dinner was always formal and dignified until the King's health had been proposed in the traditional manner. The CO remained for a while and then quietly retired, at which point youthful spirits took over.'

The first day of the month was a 'dud' because of the weather, but a patrol the next day saw some positive action, and results. At 1125 hrs, nine SE 5as – Jarvis flying top cover for the lower formation, led by Trevor Durrant – attacked a formation of seven Pfalz D IIIs and three Fokker Dr Is flying from Bray-sur-Somme. Durrant singled out a Pfalz, but both of his guns refused to fire. Burden attacked another Pfalz and sent it down in a spin, thick grey and black smoke pouring from the scout. Jarvis tackled a triplane, which turned over onto its back before falling into the clouds. He chased after his foe and saw the fighter emerge, still upside down, and crash near Martinpuich. Cyril Parry send another Pfalz down in a vertical dive, the fighter disappearing into the clouds.

This engagement had seen the unit meet with considerable success, but on the debit side, the CO, Maj Rainsford Balcombe Brown, had failed to return. He had been shot down and killed by Ltn Erich Löwenhardt, *Staffelführer* of *Jasta* 10, for his 18th victory. The loss of Balcombe Brown disorganised No 56 Sqn for the remainder of the day until David Galley took temporary command.

Edward David George Galley outside the Mess at Valheureux. Galley won an MC for his 'aggressive' ground strafing during the German offensive in March 1918. He had previously served as an observer in No 22 Sqn, flying FE2ds

On 3 May, Trevor Durrant confirmed McCudden's opinion of him as being 'very good' when he attacked a Rumpler that was heading west over Albert – it crashed at Pozières. Some 15 minutes then passed before another Rumpler was seen, flying at just 1000 ft over Aveluy Wood. Irwin, Atkinson and Durrant all attacked this machine, with the latter pilot going first. After a short burst from both Durrant's guns, which then stopped, the Rumpler dived away, followed by Irwin and Atkinson, who were both firing. The aircraft crashed at Mantaban-de-Picarde.

Twenty minutes later the trio found another Rumpler at 16,000 ft over Bertincourt. Durrant eventually attacked this machine over nearby Beaucourt, when a burst of 200 rounds either killed or wounded the observer. Durrant's guns then stopped again and Atkinson took over the attack. Despite the pilot taking evasive action, the Rumpler began to smoke, and it went down in a slow but unsteady dive. It was last seen at 2000 ft southeast of Bapaume, 'still going down very unsteadily'. Durrant was awarded the first Rumpler as destroyed, and he, Irwin and Atkinson shared the other two, one as crashed and the other as out of control.

That same day Capt Abraham Cuffe arrived to take command of A Flight. Cuffe, a Canadian, had previously seen action with No 32 Sqn during 1917, scoring four victories. On 5 May, the new CO arrived in the form of Maj Euan James Warren Gilchrist, who had served with some distinction in No 60 Sqn for six months in 1916 until he had been injured

Henry John 'Hank' Burden outside the Mess at Valheureux. Burden scored 16 victories with the squadron and was awarded a DSO and a DFC

in a crash. In the final analysis, Euan Gilchrist was to emerge as the finest of No 56 Sqn's wartime commanding officers.

Weather conditions were 'impossible' for the next two days, but on the morning of 9 May, Galley's flight attacked a Rumpler over Achiet-le-Grande, his fire sending it down diving steeply and emitting smoke. On the evening of 10 May, Cuffe and Jarvis led their flights off from Valheureux at 1840 hrs. Cuffe dropped out of the formation with engine trouble, leaving Cyril Parry to assume command.

At 1950 hrs the latter pilot saw a formation of 14 Albatros scouts, with ten below his flight and four at the same level. Parry turned the SE 5as west, climbed to 14,000 ft and attacked the top formation. Seeing that Burdette Harmon – who had ignored Parry's leadership and attacked the lower formation – was in trouble, Parry left his opponent, but was too late to save Harmon, whose SE 5a was already breaking up under enemy fire 'like a burst feather pillow'. It finally hit the ground south of the River Somme. Burden then engaged one of Harmon's attackers. The green and white Albatros that had just claimed the British scout caught fire moments later when hit by Parry's rounds, and it too crashed close by the Somme.

Parry, whose guns were out of action, was attacked by an enemy scout, its fire smashing both weapons. The Albatros then roared over Parry's head at a distance 'of about four feet'. The British pilot was now alone, and he convinced himself that he had lost the entire flight to the German scouts. However, when Parry landed at Valheureux he was astonished to see Gilchrist throwing his hat in the air, delighted that the flight had 'got some Huns'! Burden, when asked by Parry why he had left the fight, explained that a bullet had shot away the tip of his propeller, causing the engine to vibrate alarmingly. Parry thought that his own SE 5a was not too badly damaged, but upon walking over to it, he saw that the scout was terribly knocked about. Indeed, the damage was so serious that it had drawn a crowd of observers from his old battalion, the Royal Welch Fusiliers.

On 13 May an LVG was destroyed over Hamel, Durrant firing 100 rounds into it before the aircraft finally crashed onto the railway line southwest of Beaucourt. This LVG, possibly from *Fl Abt (A) 235*, gave Durrant his eighth victory.

Three days later, the squadron lost one of its most popular and promising pilots. In the last patrol of the day, Louis Jarvis led C Flight over the front, with Trevor Durrant, who had been promoted to captain and given command of B Flight that very day, leading his new command above and behind Jarvis' SE 5as. Forty minutes after crossing the lines, six Fokker Dr Is were sighted northeast of Le Sars. Durrant and his flight, thinking they were supported by C Flight, attacked the triplanes northeast of Albert. Eugene Macdonald was engaged by two of the Dr Is, and as he zoomed away, he saw an SE 5a going down in flames, which he recognised as Trevor Durrant's machine. Macdonald was hit in the engine by fire from one of the triplanes and force-landed away from base. He later recalled, 'I felt very bitter about this tragic patrol. Trevor Durrant was a very dear friend of mine'.

The loss of Durrant delivered a very heavy blow to the squadron. In addition to being a first class fighter pilot with 11 victories to his name, he was also extremely popular. Macdonald was to write of him, 'Trevor Durrant has held a place in my memory for the last 50 years as the finest Englishman I ever knew'. Gilchrist wrote a long letter to Durrant's parents, ending with, 'I really cannot speak too highly of your son – either personally or as a fighter and excellent patrol leader. His place in the squadron will be very hard to fill. We all join in sympathy with you in

Trevor Durrant, seen here in an SE 5a, was killed on the very day he became the B Flight commander. Durrant had previously served as an observer in No 55 Sqn, where he shared in a victory with his pilot. Durrant joined No 56 Sqn on 7 December 1917, and scored a further ten victories prior to his death

your anxiety, and hope with you that, after all, he may be a prisoner'. Sadly Durrant was not a prisoner. He lies now in Danzig Alley, the British cemetery at Mametz, having become the 13th victory of Ltn Hans Kirschtstein of *Jasta* 6.

Many indecisive actions were fought over the next few days. Gilchrist, who had been impressed with Parry's coolness in taking over command of the flight on 10 May, assigned him to lead A Flight in an unofficial capacity until his posting to No 60 Sqn as a flight commander on 1 July. In the coming months, Parry was to amply justify Gilchrist's judgement.

On 22 May, Parry led his flight across the lines south of Arras and attacked a pair of enemy two-seaters. He and Macdonald shot at one of the enemy machines, which went down in a fast glide. Returning later, Macdonald saw the wreckage of a two-seater near Arras, but Gilchrist would only award an indecisive classification to the victory.

Valheureux was bombed on the night of 24/25 May, prompting American pilot Owen Holleran to comment in his diary 'his work was very bad. He did no damage, save a few more holes in the landing ground'.

There were many combats over the remaining days of the month, intermittently interrupted by some bad weather, but no decisive victories were gained. Crowe flew the last patrol of the month, which was categorised as a Special Mission by the squadron. He saw no enemy aeroplanes, but dived and attacked a goods train standing just outside Bihucourt, its steam up, about to leave for Bapaume. The engine driver and his fireman leapt down and ran for cover. Crowe met no ground fire during this attack but was heavily 'Archied' on his way back to the lines.

The heavy fighting in the German offensives on the Chemin-des-Dames front during the last days of May had abated, but enemy forces were gathering for their next attack, between Noyon and Montdidier, to the north of No 56 Sqn's area of operations. German air strength was duly concentrated on this front too.

Despite the continuance of the fine weather, which enabled the squadron to fly regular patrols during the first week of June, no material results – in the shape of enemy aeroplanes destroyed – were gained until the 7th of the month, when there was a change in pace, and luck.

Parry led A Flight off the ground at 0820 hrs. Crossing the lines at 11,000 ft over Albert, three enemy two-seaters were seen – one over Fricourt at 3000 ft and two others over Grévillers at 4000 ft, all flying westwards. Parry made for the pair, catching them over Puisieux. The enemy pilots turned east, but as they were passing over Achiet-le-Petit Parry got on the tail of one and fired a short burst. The German machine began to go down, the gunner firing at Boger, who was also attacking. Parry followed, fired another burst and the two-seater erupted in flames and crashed southeast of the village. This machine was from *Fl Abt (A)* 211, and Uffz Kirsten and Gefr Mertens were both killed.

Twenty-five minutes later, Parry sighted another pair of two-seaters. He dived to attack these and closed to within 30 yards, his fire killing or wounding the observer, who slumped forwards over the pilot. The two-seater went down to crash northeast of Grévillers. Parry quickly turned his attention to its companion, firing the remainder of his ammunition into it from a range of just 20 yards. The observer collapsed over the side of his cockpit and the enemy pilot dived away, followed by Parry, who had

Owen Cobb Holleran commanded A Flight from 11 August 1918 to 15 September 1918, when he was shot down and taken prisoner

no more ammunition. Macdonald took up the attack and the enemy machine finally force-landed. All three SE 5as followed this last two-seater down and were considerably shot about by ground fire. Burden jubilantly recorded in his diary 'Parry got one two-seater crashed, one in flames, and one driven down this morning before breakfast'.

That night a party went into Le Touquet to celebrate Parry's victories, the first to be scored since 16 May, and it was hoped they had ended a lean period in the squadron's fortunes. Fifty years later, Parry still had vivid memories of the party, especially that he was knocked down the stairs of a hotel by a burly MP when slightly tipsy for the first time in his life!

On 10 June an old friend arrived. After eight months instructing at No 1 School of Aerial Fighting at Ayr, in Scotland, Gerald Maxwell rejoined No 56 Sqn for a refresher course in frontline operations. He was eager to get back to active service flying, and Crowe took him out in the evening to show him the position of the frontlines – considerably altered since Maxwell had last fought over the area in the spring of 1917.

That same evening another 'old boy' arrived. James McCudden, having flown the first production Sopwith Snipe to France for evaluation trials, had taken the opportunity to visit the unit. Maxwell and McCudden took off together on the morning of 12 June. No 56 Sqn's Operational Record

Book makes no mention of McCudden flying any patrols during his visit, but Maxwell's diary entry reads, 'Did a show with McCudden in the morning. Went up to 18,500 ft for two hours. Felt very ill in consequence. Saw nothing'.

To the delight of both Maxwell and McCudden, 13 June was a fine, warm day, and they both took off at 0605 hrs. McCudden, flying Irwin's Viper-powered SE 5a, commented in his logbook 'very nice machine'. Maxwell's diary records, 'Did a topping show in morning. Self and McCudden attacked four different two-seaters which we filled with lead but did not get down'.

McCudden did not take these failures as philosophically as Maxwell. On the evidence of his camera gun records at Turnberry, he knew his marksmanship was as good as ever, and a test of Irwin's guns at the butts confirmed his suspicion – the guns were hopelessly misaligned. McCudden was 'hopping mad' that such a fundamental rule of his teaching had so soon been ignored, and he severely reprimanded Irwin for not having his guns properly aligned and sighted. McCudden returned to England later in the day, no doubt annoyed that he had failed to add to his score.

A strong force of ten SE 5as took off at 1030 hrs on the 13th. After attacking a pair of two-seaters, the British scouts were in turn bounced by a formation of Fokker Dr Is over Le Sars. Copeland fired at one, reporting 'got onto him and fired a burst of 40 rounds, when he turned over and went down obviously out of control'. Cyril Stenning was harder pressed. Although hit in the radiator and petrol tank by an accurate burst from an enemy pilot, Stenning turned under his attacker, pulled down his Lewis gun and fired a full drum at point blank range. The triplane spun away. Stenning headed home and eventually crashed a short distance from Valheureux in his badly shot up SE 5a. He also had four bullet holes in his flying suit. Stenning was considerably shaken by the episode, but in some consolation he was awarded a victory for the Fokker triplane thanks to the unit receiving confirmation from several AA batteries, which also confirmed another success for Boger.

The Fokker Dr 1 was not a fast machine, but its triplane layout gave the scout a remarkable rate of climb and made it highly manoeuvrable – both attributes that made the scout ideally suited to a close-in fighting style of combat. The Dr I was temporarily withdrawn from service with the *Jagdstaffeln* at the end of October 1917 because of various structural faults, but it was in full operational use again by the end of November 1917, reaching peak strength in April 1918 when 171 examples were at the front

Cyril Brownlow Stenning served with the squadron from 13 March until 29 September 1918, when he was invalided to hospital

There was no flying on 14 June, as the unit had six officers on the sick list with Spanish 'flu. Stenning was also sent home on leave, Holleran commenting, 'This is a good thing considering the way he was shot up yesterday'. Two days later, No 56 Sqn suffered its first casualty for a month. Fraser Tarbutt, who had just returned from leave with news of his plans to marry an American film actress in Canada during his next leave in July, was killed in an afternoon patrol. He was reported last seen diving after a pair of two-seaters, but Macdonald recalled seeing Tarbutt dip his right wings and turn back early from the patrol. He had fired no signal to indicate a reason for leaving the formation, and when Macdonald next looked he saw the Canadian's SE 5a disintegrate;

'I could not see any enemy aeroplanes, we had not been shelled by "Archie" and we were flying too high for machine gun fire to be effective. The weather was good, as was the visibility. I got the impression that Tarbutt had blacked out and gone down with his throttle full open. He was a very big fine fellow, not the boisterous type, but quiet and unassuming, calm and steadfast. I had flown in formation with him on many occasions, and had great confidence in his courage and ability. His disappearance appeared to be unaccountable – a tragic end to the life of a very gallant fighter pilot. Some things are indelibly imprinted on one's mind, and for me, the sight of Tarbutt going west was one of them.'

Fraser Coventry Tarbutt, seen here in an SE 5a, was killed in action on 16 June 1918

During the remainder of this patrol, Maxwell, in spite of having a loose cowling, fought a two-seater for some time near Hamelincourt until a burst from close range caused the enemy pilot to dive steeply away. He then landed to have the cowling secured. Returning to the lines, Maxwell attacked a two-seater over Arras, shooting it down in flames to crash near Wancourt at 1935 hrs. Ltn Spack and Vfw Jockwer of *Fl Abt (A) 284* were both killed. AA batteries confirmed both of these victories, which took Maxwell's tally to 22 – these were his first aerial successes since 30 September 1917.

On 18 June Parry led his flight in an action that was to earn him a Distinguished Flying Cross (DFC). The patrol had seen a formation of Albatros scouts patrolling ten miles east of the lines, and initially the enemy fighters headed for the six SE 5as until the lead pilot changed his mind and turned away. They quickly lost height and landed at their aerodrome at Suzanne. From 3000 ft, just east of the enemy airfield, Parry dived and opened fire on one of the 'V' Strutters that was still airborne. The German pilot immediately dived and landed a mile from his aerodrome. Parry was prevented from following up this advantage when he came under attack from the remaining enemy fighters that had yet to land.

After seeing Burden attack an Albatros that quickly crashed, Parry fired a red light to reform the patrol, intending to lead it in a strafing run over

Cyril Parry was A Flight commander from 18 May to 1 July 1918. Here, he is wearing his DFC ribbon with the original horizontal purple and white stripes. which were later changed to diagonal. Parry was posted to No 60 Sqn as a flight commander of 1 July 1918, but was seriously injured in a crash exactly four weeks later. He survived the war to become a highly successful businessman, and in 1968 Parry hosted a dinner party for the remaining members of No 56 Sqn

the enemy aerodrome. By then, however, the other SE 5a pilots were too busy fighting. Seeing one of the enemy pilots closing in behind Herbert Mulroy's machine, Parry rejoined the fight and shot the Albatros off his squadronmate's tail – it was seen to crash by Burden. Parry then saw that Molyneux was also about to be attacked and went to his assistance, driving off his attackers. Spotting two more enemy scouts taking off from Suzanne, Parry dived and attacked them at 400 ft over the aerodrome, but he was forced to turn away when his Lewis gun jammed and the CC gear of his Vickers failed.

The other members of the flight had also been busy. Boger sent an Albatros down in a vertical dive, while Burden, after despatching a fighter in a spin, zoomed away to change his Lewis gun drum. He then fired from close range at another enemy scout that broke up at 1000 ft. On his way back to the lines, Burden attacked two balloons and saw Mulroy's machine sustain a direct hit from a *KFlakBatterrie* of the German 17th Army over Aveluy Wood.

Following this action, Maj Gilchrist wrote to Wing HQ recommending Cyril Parry for a decoration;

'Sir, I beg to bring to your notice the very gallant work done by this officer since he joined the Squadron on the 4th of January this year. Since this date he has taken part in 55 offensive patrols and several Special Missions, on all of which he has shown great determination and gallantry.'

Gilchrist then went on to summarise some of Parry's exploits, ending with a detailed description of that morning's fight over the enemy aerodrome. He ended his recommendation, 'The moral effect produced by his dashing leadership on this patrol must be very great, for many spectators had gathered on the aerodrome to watch the fight. I feel that the services he has rendered are deserving of recognition'.

Cyril Parry, referring to his part in the history of No 56 Sqn, described himself to the writer as 'an also-ran in a stable of good horses'. It was the quality of these 'also-rans' which made the strength of the RAF in 1918 so formidable.

The weather was dull and overcast on 22 June when Maxwell visited No 56 Sqn's old aerodrome at Vert Galant – a place full of nostalgic memories for the ace. His diary records 'went over to see the old garden at Vert Galant'. As he looked at the remains of the garden that Albert Ball had so hopefully cultivated in the spring of 1917, it must have seemed to Maxwell that more than just a year had passed. His squadronmates Ball, Prothero, Kay, Sloley, Rhys Davids, Barlow and 'Dickie' Maybery had all perished since then.

NEW OPPONENT

During the evening of 27 June, No 56 Sqn's pilots had their first combats with a new German fighter when they attacked three Fokker D VIIs over Morcourt. Maxwell fired at one which 'wobbled a bit and dived, pursued by Lts Parry and Irwin'. Three Fokker Dr Is then attempted to attack Parry and Irwin, but Maxwell dived at them from out of the sun. 'Got on the tail of one enemy aircraft without him seeing me. I got to within about ten yards' range – so close I could see his face and goggles – and fired both guns'. The triplane, which had a black and white check around its fuselage, side slipped, then spun slowly down.

Right
The Pfalz D III entered service with the *Jagdstaffeln* in August 1917. Although not favoured by German pilots, at least one, Paul Bäumer of *Jasta* 'Boelcke', flew the Pfalz with great élan

The Fokker D VII, which entered service with the *Jagdstaffeln* in April 1918, was the finest fighter aeroplane produced by the Germans in World War 1. Strong, fast, manoeuvrable and easy to fly, the Fokker had the apparent facility to transform a poor pilot into a good one. The first Mercedes-powered examples gave the pilots of No 56 Sqn little trouble, but with the appearance of the BMW IIIa-powered version, it became an extremely formidable opponent. Indeed, in this form the D VII was arguably the finest fighter aeroplane to see frontline service with any of the combatants

The next day started badly. In an early morning patrol over Miraumont, Allan Garrett was lightly wounded and forced to land by fire from *KFlakbaterrie 7*, his demise being credited to Vfw Neumann. In the evening Maxwell led a large force of 11 SE 5as on the last patrol of the day, which saw a great deal of fighting. The fighters first attacked a large formation of Fokker D VIIs, Albatros D Vs and Pfalz D IIIs over Dompierre, sparking off the biggest dogfight the squadron had been in for some time. Holleran recorded in his diary;

'We were going along at about 17,000 ft when Maxwell made war signals and dove under a bank of clouds. We came out all scattered among 35 or 40 Huns – Pfalz, Fokker D VIIs and Albatri. I suppose they must have thought it was raining British machines.'

Holleran stayed close to the cloud cover, picking his opponent, but he saw his close friend Bill Hazen going down with three enemy

machines on his tail. Holleran, throwing caution to the wind, dived after Hazen's attackers;

'Two of the Huns saw me coming and their ambitions evaporated. They beat it. Unfortunately, another fellow saw me coming also and stood on his tail and put a burst of about 100 rounds into my bus, one of which connected with my left shin. I thought for an instance my foot was gone. I pulled the "U-boat up onto her back pronto". He was forced to dive under me and I came out about 50 ft from his tail and instinctively gave him both guns. His head simply disappeared in a flash. My machine was a wreck, so I hit out for home, steering on the sun.'

Holleran's wound was only a light one, and he was excused duty for five days. On the bottom of his combat report Gilchrist noted that Holleran's ammunition, hit by enemy fire, was still smoking after he had landed.

As a result of this patrol, Maxwell, Hazen, Crowe and Irwin were all awarded victories, but Harry Austin had been shot down and captured after his machine was targeted by ace Ltn d R Emil Thuy of *Jasta* 28 –

William Roy Irwin in his SE 5a. A Canadian from Ripley, Ontario, he served with No 56 Sqn from 29 January to 15 September 1918, when he was wounded in action. Irwin scored 11 victories while with the squadron, earning him a DFC and Bar

Austin was his 23rd victim. Several pilots noticed that the D VIIs in this fight had distinctive black and white squares painted onto their fuselages.

There was little flying on 29 June, Maxwell recording in his diary 'Very dud. No flying. Went for a ride in a tank'. During the course of the day two American pilots arrived at the squadron in the form of Paul Winslow and Tommy Herbert. The former confessed to his diary 'I think we both landed on our feet, as this is the top squadron in the RAF'.

Cyril Crowe and Bill Boger gained the last victory in June on the 30th when they attacked four LVGs over Courcelles at 1045 hrs. One turned away from Crowe's fire and Boger then attacked it, causing the LVG to burst into flames and crash just east of Logest Wood. This was possibly a machine from *Fl Abt (A)* 284, who reported that Ltn d Rs Bertram and Böhme had been killed over Achiet-le-Grand.

June had been another month of varied success for No 56 Sqn. Several pilots were now developing into useful and aggressive aviators, and although the squadron had fewer high scorers than in its past, some names began to appear with increasing frequency in the unit's victory list during the next two months. In the first half of July the squadron was to lose its best flight commanders not from enemy action but in postings to No 60 Sqn – Cyril Parry on 1 July, followed by Crowe on the 10th and John Doyle on the 16th.

July 1918 saw the Germans launch their last attempt to bring the war to a successful conclusion, but Gen Ludendorff's final offensive, *Friedensturm*, which commenced on 15 July, was brought to a standstill in just three days. The German High Command now realised that the war was lost, and a worthwhile peace settlement could only be achieved by fighting grimly on until the last of its resources had been expended. To the hardpressed squadrons of the RAF, these strategic considerations were unknown. The *Luftstreitkräfte* fought superbly until the bitter end, and during the final five months of the war the RAF suffered heavy casualties.

For No 56 Sqn, July was reasonably successful, starting well with two victories on the first day of the month. Over Aveluy Wood, a bright red Fokker Dr I spun down on Gerald Maxwell, firing as it came. He took evasive action and the triplane dived away, only to be attacked by Crowe. 'The triplane fell to pieces in my Aldis sight. I was then at about 3500 ft over Thiepval'. This was possibly the aircraft flown by Vfw Georg Schalk of *Jasta* 34b, who was killed over Albert. Crowe then destroyed a Fokker D VII, which crashed northeast of Albert.

Four days later, over Dompierre, Maxwell shot a Fokker D VII down in flames, confirmed by pilots of No 41 Sqn. On 6 July Leslie Franklin and Eugene Macdonald each accounted for a Hannover over Tilloy-les-Mofflaines, AA batteries confirming that one had crashed and the other one driven right down. On the evening of 9 July, the squadron was stunned to hear that Maj James McCudden had been killed in a flying accident while on his way to take command of No 60 Sqn at Filescamp Farm. The following afternoon the squadron attended his funeral in Auxi-le-Chateau. The ceremony angered many of those present, with Burden commenting 'it was poorly arranged and rushed through'. Winslow recorded;

'All of 60 were there, together with Gen Salmond and some members of other squadrons. The ceremony made my blood boil – all in Latin, mumbled so that even if one knew the language, he couldn't have heard it. Nothing human in it at all, and far from impressive. Richthofen – an

William Otway Boger was a Canadian from Winnipeg who had previously served as an observer with No 11 Sqn prior to joining No 56 Sqn on 24 May 1918. Boger was awarded five victories before he was killed in action on 10 August 1918

enemy – had a far better funeral, and if anyone deserved a real memorial, it was McCudden.'

In an early morning patrol on 14 July, while attacking an LVG over Hendecourt, Leslie Franklin was shot down in flames. He was awarded to Ltn Enke and Vfw Leopold (unit unknown) and buried by the side of the road to Mory.

Despite the unsettled weather conditions, some patrols were flown over the next seven days, but with no success. On 22 July Gerald Maxwell came to the end of his refresher course and left for England. Winslow wrote, 'Saw Capt Maxwell and Majority Crowe off in a blaze of glory – the former was one of the nicest men I have ever met'.

On 24 July Boger shot down a Pfalz D III in flames out of a formation of nine – this was Ltn Hofig of *Jasta* 37, who was killed. It was also the last action fought by No 56 Sqn in July. During the remaining days of the month the unit practised low-level bombing in preparation for the Allied offensives, which was due to begin on 8 August. An extensive bombing and close support programme had been assigned to the RAF, part of which called for low-level attacks on German aerodromes. One such mission was attempted on 30 July, but it was aborted by bad weather.

LAST OFFENSIVES

For No 56 Sqn, August commenced with an attack on the enemy aerodrome at Epinoy on the 1st. This mission had been carefully planned. The enemy aerodrome straddled a road, and the Camels of No 3 Sqn, which were leading the attack, were allocated buildings to the south of the road. No 56 Sqn was told to target sheds and aircraft north of the road, with each flight being given a specific area to attack. Both units were to approach the aerodrome at low level.

The raid proved to be an unqualified success. Led by Maj Gilchrist, the SE 5as attacked along the length of the enemy sheds at a height of just 200 ft. Gilchrist hit a workshop, setting it on fire, while Boger, who was flying alongside his CO, was told to knock out enemy machine gun posts. He duly fired at the crews as they ran to man their guns, Gilchrist later commenting, 'Boger undoubtedly saved those coming afterwards from any machine gun fire'.

The scene over the aerodrome was one of utter confusion, Camels and SE 5as barely avoiding collisions. After dropping his bombs, Burden attacked machines lined up outside the hangars, setting a black aircraft on fire. He also saw another pilot destroy a second aeroplane. Winslow's bombs flattened a hangar, and he also attacked the enemy living quarters. He noted, 'It was war and it was Hell, but it was also very funny. I actually laughed at the antics on the ground'. Gilchrist attacked a Pfalz, leaving it in flames, before he turned for the lines nursing a badly running engine.

Ace Ltn Rudolf Stark, who was *Staffelführer* of *Jasta* 35b at Epinoy, wrote about the raid in his autobiography *Wings of War*;

'One of *Jagdstaffel* 23's hangers went up in flames and burnt to the ground with seven machines inside it. The bullets rained like hail on the roofs. The English were the most amazingly impertinent, and they hardly knew how to find outlets for their arrogance.'

Stark and his pilots could do little but watch. A telephone call to another *Jasta* brought no response. 'But the storm vanished as quickly as it came. Up went a Very light as a signal and off went all the machines to vanish in the west'. The attack had lasted just ten minutes. In that time No 56 Sqn had dropped 44 20-lb Cooper bombs and expended the greater part of its ammunition. Including the escorts for Nos 3 and 56 Sqns (SE 5as from No 60 Sqn, as well as Sopwith Dolphins and Bristol Fighters flying above the action), some 65 machines had participated in this raid, and all had returned home.

Although the weather was bad, with low cloud, mist and rain, several patrols were flown without incident until 4 August, when Boger led A Flight in an attack on six Pfalz D IIIs southeast of Bray. Thomas Herbert fired at one Pfalz, which was seen to break up. Boger then saw seven Fokker D VIIs 'coming up fast', and he fired a red light to break off the action. Winslow and Stenning, although getting away safely, were roughly handled by the Fokkers.

The Allied offensive opened on 8 August. No 56 Sqn, although a part of the Fifth Army, was ordered to assist operations over the Fourth Army

Accepted as 'one of the boys' by his pilots, Maj Euan James Leslie Warren 'Gilly' Gilchrist commanded No 56 Sqn from 2 May until 17 December 1918. Like many others, he went against official orders that squadron commanders should not fly on active operations and undertook many patrols, including the unit's successful raids on enemy aerodromes. Gilchrist was liked by all the pilots in No 56 Sqn, with the only adverse remark against him being that he was 'a bit of a fire-eater'

109

Americans and Canadians with the squadron circa 1 August 1918. Standing, from left to right, are R H Ellis, G A Elmslie, P Winslow, C B Stenning, W O Boger, T J Herbert, T D Hazen and J K Blair, and seated, again from left to right, are W E Borncamp and V H Hervey

front, and therefore found itself in the thick of the air fighting east of Amiens. No actions were fought in the morning, but an afternoon patrol, supported by Bristol Fighters, engaged a large number of Fokker D VIIs and Pfalz D IIIs northeast of Chaulnes. During the fighting 'Sambo' Irwin shot down a D VII in flames and Tommy Herbert caused another to crash. The latter pilot was then wounded by one of the Fokkers. Hit in the knee, and with his petrol tank holed, Herbert managed to land, but fainted from loss of blood as his SE 5a hit the ground. He was extracted from his machine by Canadian soldiers, and when Herbert came round he was on a stretcher carried by German PoWs. Not unnaturally, he concluded that he had been taken prisoner!

Burden, Winslow and Herbert enjoy a break from the action during a swimming party on the Somme

In Paul Winslow's words, 10 August was 'a gala day for the Royal Air Force'. Hank Burden led the first patrol of the day, shooting down a Fokker D VII to crash north of Suzanne, and a long burst at a second scout sent the fighter crashing in a field by a river east of the village. In a later fight, Burden shot another Fokker D VII to pieces over Puzeaux, bringing his total for the patrol to three destroyed. Herbert Allen failed to return from this action, however, having been shot down and killed by Uffz Lohrmann of *Jasta* 42.

Both flights that performed the next patrol also met with some success. Over Marchélpot, Irwin sent a D VII down out of control and had another burst into flames under his fire. The top flight was not so lucky, however. William Boger, the flight commander and five-victory ace, was shot down and killed, and Herbert Flintoft was forced to land in enemy territory, where he was taken prisoner. The squadron, shaken by its losses of the morning, nevertheless consolidated its earlier successes with another five victories during the evening patrols.

Two flights had taken off, and again over Puzeaux Burden added to his victories of the morning, shooting down another two Fokker D VIIs – the first crashed near Morchain and the second near Cizancourt. Irwin, Stenning and Winslow had also all scored. Irwin's Fokker crashed north of Roye, Stenning's opponent fell away out of control and Winslow sent another of the D VIIs down in a slow spin, which developed into an uncontrolled dive. He commented 'I've never felt so bucked in my life'. Burden's two Fokker D VIIs brought his total for the day to five, and his overall tally to ten.

On 12 August, Burden added to his score with another Fokker D VII out of control, confirmed by William Irwin, who downed another. Harold Molyneux fired at a third Fokker, which crashed in a field. Irwin pulled down his Lewis and fired into another of the enemy machines, which was seen to crash by Burden, who had already shot down yet

Paul Stewart Winslow served with No 56 Sqn from 29 June until 12 September 1918, when he was transferred to the US Army Air Service

Harold Arthur Sydney Molyneux was also a Canadian, hailing from Toronto. He served as C Flight commander from 7 to 21 October 1918, when he was invalided to hospital. By then Molyneux had scored five victories and been awarded a DFC

another Fokker, blue smoke coming from its cockpit before it burst into flames. Burden then attacked a third D VII head on. The enemy machine stalled, fell out of control and was seen to spin into the ground. On landing it was found that American pilot Robert Ellis had also scored, bringing No 56 Sqn's total to seven Fokker D VIIs destroyed. Burden wrote in his diary '20 Huns for the squadron in four days'.

It was misty all day on 13 August, but Burden and Holleran took out their flights in the morning. After a skirmish with Fokker D VIIs, which his diary colourfully describes as 'nearly peed on by seven Fokkers', Burden shot down a DFW, which hit the ground in the hamlet of Gueudecourt. An evening patrol on 15 August saw another victory for Hank Burden. He dived to attack an LVG over Croisilles, but before he could fire the aircraft flew straight into the ground near Mory. Molyneux commented 'One two-seater crashed from fright'.

The squadron was now operating on the Third Army front, where aerial activity was much reduced and the weather was not good. This meant that there were no more victories to be had until the 19th, when Holleran took out a patrol in the morning and ran into a large formation of 43 enemy fighters – Fokker D VIIs and Dr Is. He later wrote, 'There was nothing for it so we ran'! All the SE 5as escaped with the exception of Bill Hazen, who was shot down and killed by Vfw Josef Mai of *Jasta* 5 – his third victory on this date, taking his overall tally to 23. Holleran, angry at

H A S Molyneux poses in SE 5a 'X'

being chased 'across half of France', later attacked a pair of Hannovers northeast of Arras. Turning to evade Holleran's fire, the Hannovers collided and crashed near Biache.

On 21 August, as part of the Allied offensive to recover the Arras to Albert railway, No 56 Sqn carried out extensive attacks on ground targets. During the day, Robert Ellis was shot down by ground fire and taken prisoner, while Noel Bishop crash-landed on the British side of the lines. Finally, Burden's SE 5a, marked *Maybe*, was so badly damaged that it was written off strength.

The following day, after another morning of ground strafing, a normal Close Offensive Patrol was flown at noon. Burden shot down a Fokker D VII with diagonal yellow and black stripes on its tailplane, the enemy machine crashing a mile northwest of Péronne. On 23 August the popular little Noel Bishop returned after his force-landing of two days previously. Burden's diary reads 'Bishop got back from hospital today, and he was mad because someone had stolen the bullet that had lodged between his ribs'.

Ground strafing and aerial fighting continued over the next few days, and two pilots were lost on the 24th – Douglas Collier fell to Vfw Könnecke of *Jasta* 5 and Australian Henry Roberts was shot down and taken prisoner. On 29 August, Holleran recorded 'Rain all day and no flying. I hope it stays so for three or four days because the whole crowd are getting nervous'. However, the rain failed to stop the war, and although patrols were flown on the last two days of the month, there were no further gains or losses.

So ended August 1918. The tempo of the war was increasing, and it had been a bad month for the squadron, with 11 casualties – the highest number in a single month since the squadron had been in France. September was to be no better as the fierce air fighting accompanying the ground offensive continued unabated.

FINAL MONTHS

On 1 September No 56 Sqn lost one its finest patrol leaders when Henry John 'Hank' Burden left for Home Establishment. Burden, a Canadian

By the summer of 1918, with the influx of Americans and Canadians in No 56 Sqn, baseball had replaced football and rugby as the squadron game. The British members of the unit regarded this with a certain amount of amused tolerance. To them, it was merely a grown up game of rounders. The squadron's baseball team was comprised of, from left to right, Flintoft (the only Englishman in the team), Ellis, Irwin, Thompson, Hazen, Winslow, Burden, Herbert and Boger from Toronto, had served for six-and-a-half months with the unit, received a DFC and a DSO and been credited with 16 victories. That same day Harold Molyneux claimed the first success of the month when he sent a Fokker D VII down out of control south of Reincourt.

On 2 September an offensive was opened by the First and Third Armies against the Drocourt-Quéant switch line. No 56 Sqn flew patrols and ground strafed throughout the day, and had William Strathearn shot down and taken prisoner north of Douai. In a morning fight with Fokker D VIIs over Etaign on the 3rd, Irwin shot down one, which hit the ground south of Rumancourt. He then went to the aid of Alfred Vickers, who was being attacked by another Fokker. Irwin fired at point blank range and the scout burst into flames and crashed west of Haynecourt, but he had been too late to save Vickers, who was later reported killed. Henry Chubb had also sent a Fokker down in flames. In an escort to DH 4s in the afternoon, the SE 5as broke up an attack by Fokker D VIIs, and American pilot Larry Bowen shot one down out of control. Its demise was confirmed by a DH 4 crew.

That evening Capt Duncan Grinnell-Milne reported for duty. He was no ordinary pilot arriving at the front straight from flying school, however. Grinnell-Milne had been captured in December 1915 after his BE 2 (of No 16 Sqn) had been shot down over enemy lines, and following several unsuccessful attempts he had finally escaped in April 1918. Once retrained as a fighter pilot, he was posted back to France, but was then incarcerated in another 'prison camp' – in this case a pilots' pool.

Grinnell-Milne's name was near the bottom of a list of dozens of pilots waiting to be posted to a squadron, but a sleight of hand involving a spilt bottle of ink and the list, with an ever helpful Grinnell-Milne dictating a new copy to the typist, resulted in his name now heading the list! He felt sorry for those pilots who had been waiting three weeks for a posting, 'but I had been waiting for nearly three years'.

The air fighting and ground strafing continued. On 4 September, after patrols had bombed and ground-strafed, Maj Gilchrist destroyed a balloon over Noyelles.

A violent storm on the evening of 7 September washed out all flying for the next three days. Holleran wrote, 'Three days of glorious weather, hard, steady unceasing rain which has made it impossible for us to get off the ground. Lord help the infantry though'. In fact there was little flying until 15 September, when the squadron returned to operations and lost three pilots.

In an early patrol, fighting Fokker D VIIs, Irwin was wounded in the side. On returning to Valheureux he was sent to hospital. That afternoon the squadron bombed the enemy aerodrome at Estourmel, which the Germans called Boistrancourt. As in the raid on Epinoy, Gilchrist again led the attack, bombing the sheds and machine gunning aircraft and personnel. All the pilots pressed home their attacks, firing at sheds, hangars, gun emplacements and aircraft on the ground. On his way back, Holleran was shot down by ground fire and taken prisoner. While attacking a train near Estourmel, Larry Bowen, the popular American, was killed by ground fire, crashing in the village. It had been a bad day for the squadron. Both Holleran and Irwin were valuable flight commanders, and Bowen had shown great promise as a fighter pilot.

Laurence Grant Bowen was an American from Michigan who moved to Toronto, Canada, so that he could enlist in the RFC. Bowen was shot down and killed by ground fire on 15 September 1918

Noel Frederick Bishop was killed in action on 16 September 1918

These casualties were followed by another the next afternoon when, in combat over Havrincourt Wood, Molyneux shot a Fokker D VII to pieces but Noel Bishop was killed by Ltn Marcard of *Jasta* 26. On 22 September the squadron suffered its seventh casualty of the month when John Gunn was shot down by anti-aircraft fire, one of the wings breaking off of his SE 5a when it suffered a direct hit. Miraculously, Gunn survived the crash uninjured and was captured.

Two days later, Chubb shot down a Fokker D VII, which crashed near Sailly, and Molyneux claimed another that hit the ground just south of the Arras-to-Cambrai road. During the combat, Frank Sedore had been wounded in the foot, resulting in him being taken to hospital upon his return to base. In an evening patrol, Chubb was awarded a Fokker D VII as out of control.

In a patrol on the 27th, while escorting ground-strafing Camels, Chubb shot down another D VII, which crashed north of Cambrai. Jack Pouchet also shot down a Fokker northeast of the town and new pilot William Clarkson claimed a third out of control. Stenning, flying in the top flight, also claimed a Fokker D VII, which crashed near Cambrai.

William Ewart Clarkson served in the squadron from 19 August 1918 until it was reduced to cadre status on 15 February 1919

Grinnell-Milne's sketch of the episode on 28 September 1918

This was a successful patrol, but George Mackenzie failed to return – he had been shot down and killed over Cambrai by Ltn Paul Bäumer of *Jasta* 'Boelcke' for his 35th victory.

On 28 September the squadron flew more low-level bombing attacks, supporting the advance of the British First and Third Armies.

Whilst participating in one of these sorties Grinnell-Milne wrote off his second SE 5a in 48 hours! After bombing a railway signal box, troops and transports, one of his bombs hit a hidden ammunition dump and the resultant explosion blew off his fighter's right-hand tailplane and elevator. The SE 5a then hit the ground in an almost vertical dive, and 'there was a ghastly noise of breaking and splintering' and Grinnell-Milne was thrown forward against his safety belt. Amazingly the scout flew on, minus its undercarriage. 'There must have been a slight fall in the ground just at that point, for had it been level or sloping up I would have crashed irremediably, and fatally', he recalled.

Gingerly trying the controls, Grinnell-Milne found that the SE 5a was somehow still flying. It was minus its undercarriage, one tip of the propeller had broken off, causing the engine to vibrate alarmingly, and the tailplane – held on by only one wire – was trailing behind it. Grinnell-Milne finally crashed his badly damaged aeroplane behind the British positions and returned to the squadron that evening.

Weather conditions grounded No 56 Sqn for the last two days of the month. It had been a bad period for the unit, with four pilots killed and three wounded in action and one in an accident. Three more had been shot down and taken prisoner. Overall, during the month of September the RAF had lost 235 aeroplanes – the highest loss rate for any month during 1918. The *Luftstreitkräfte*, despite materiel shortages, was clearly still a force to be reckoned with.

THE LAST DAYS

Suddenly, in October 1918, the German Army began to crumble in the first stages of its final disintegration. The Allied armies were poised for their last great effort. Although some aerial combats were fought during the month, No 56 Sqn's main task was one of ground attack in support of the rapidly advancing British armies. For example, on 3 October, eight SE 5as carried out attacks in the vicinity of Beauvois, Cattenièrs, Wambaix and Nergnies. Grinnell-Milne and Gilchrist were detailed to attack balloons, and south of Caudry, the latter shot one down in flames. He then strafed a car that 'looked like a Ford'. Grinnell-Milne had his usual trouble with ground fire, however, being hit in the petrol tank and twice forced to return to base for repairs.

The following day Robert Caldwell destroyed a balloon, before groundstrafing troops and gun batteries. These attacks were repeated on 5 October, when both Speaks and Grinnell-Milne destroyed balloons too, but Ivan Awde, after destroying his, was shot down by its protective guns. He managed to force-land his damaged fighter and was taken prisoner. Jack Pouchet failed to return, however, having been shot down and killed by ground fire.

Dawn on 8 October saw the opening of the second Battle of Cambrai. In support of the offensive, the squadron's pilots continued their ground attacks, with bombs and machine guns. Grinnell-Milne confessed, 'It was my fault this time. I tried too many conclusions with machine guns, which I had foolishly thought could be mastered with a few steep hard-firing dives'. Once again his SE 5a was badly hit, and although the engine escaped damage, the petrol tank was badly holed. Grinnell-Milne returned to base.

Robert Allan 'Bloody Bobs' Caldwell, 'whose field boots, however grimy his hands, were always spotless mirrors', stands by his SE 5a H693 'A'

117

American John C Speaks served with the squadron from 16 August 1918 until 14 March 1919, when he dispersed the cadre

Duncan Grinnell-Milne with the squadron transport at No 13 Wing HQ at Caudry in December 1918. 'G-M' was the squadron's last commanding officer of the war

There was no further flying until 14 October, when the squadron repeated its attacks on the now rapidly retreating German troops. The next day it was time to leave 'that quiet orchard at Valheureux', No 56 Sqn moving to a new base at Lechelle, southeast of Bapaume.

There was no further flying until the afternoon of 21 October, when the unit returned to ground attack duties. Gilchrist targeted an enemy aerodrome that was home to Halberstadts marked with bright yellow fuselages, green tails and silver and black striped top planes. Grinnell-Milne, after dropping his bombs on enemy troops, attacked a Fokker D VII. He only ceased firing at it when the scout 'had entered the ground'. On his way back to the lines, Caldwell shot down a D VII out of control near Hauntmont. These were the first aerial victories for No 56 Sqn in nearly a month, and they were tempered by the loss of Moses Winkler (a native of Laurel, Mississippi). Last seen flying east of Le Cateau, he had crash-landed his SE 5a in German-held territory and soon been taken prisoner.

Close Offensive Patrols were flown over the next five days, but no actions were fought until the morning of 27 October when five Fokker D VIIs were attacked east of Le Cateau. In the general fighting Thomas Rogers was shot down and killed. That afternoon the unit again changed aerodromes, but the frontline was now moving eastwards at such speed that No 56 Sqn was only at its new base at Esnes for two days before it was ordered to move again to La Targette.

This aerodrome was very near Boistrancourt, which had been the scene of the squadron's attack on 15 September. Soon after arriving, Johnny Speaks found the grave of his friend Larry Bowen. On a cold and misty morning, with Bill Clarkson holding a pot of white paint, Speaks sat astride the grave and painted the name and details of his fellow American on the broken propeller that served as his cross.

A patrol in the afternoon of 29 October saw a great deal of fighting with several large formations of Fokker D VIIs. In a general melee, numbering upwards of 50 aircraft, Grinnell-Milne shot down one of the Fokker fighters, which crashed near Bois l'Evéque. This victory was the last for No 56 Sqn in October.

The month had been fairly productive, and casualties had been light. A great deal of effective ground strafing and bombing had been done, although victories in the air had been few – only two and one shared with another unit, plus four balloons – but as one pilot recalled, 'It was very difficult to get a fight at all during the last weeks of the war'.

The final 11 days of hostilities saw a resurgence of air-to-air combat, however. The first 48 hours of November saw several indecisive brushes with enemy aircraft, but on the morning of the 3rd, Grinnell-Milne attacked a Fokker D VII, which dived away into the smoke of a burning factory. He followed and attacked again. Large pieces broke off the centre section of the Fokker as it began to burn, and at 500 ft the scout dived into the canal at Condé. This victory took Grinnell-Milne's tally to five, making him No 56 Sqn's final ace of the war. In the afternoon Johnny Speaks shot down a Fokker D VII over Bavai for the squadron's last victory of the conflict.

In combats on 4 November, Richard Shutes was wounded and Oliver Price was shot down and killed by Oblt Karl Bolle, *Staffelführer* of *Jasta* 'Boelcke' – this was one of four victories he claimed on this date, taking his final tally to 36. Weather conditions were now poor, and there was no flying until the 9th. Patrols were hampered by a strong west wind, and during an afternoon patrol James Crawford became the 11th victim of Ltn Rudolf Stark, *Staffelführer* of *Jasta* 35b.

On the penultimate day of hostilities, the squadron returned to ground strafing, attacking the retreating and demoralised German troops. The unit's last patrol of the war left the ground at 0630 hrs on 11 November. No enemy aeroplanes were seen and the patrol returned at 0825 hrs. The long struggle was finally over.

Six days later Euan Gilchrist went on leave, passing active command of the squadron to Grinnell-Milne. Gilchrist had been in poor health for some months, Grinnell-Milne writing;

'He refused to give up. His was the sort of courage that, however hackneyed the word, can only be described as indomitable. For the sake of his squadron, for the sake of us, his pilots, he was determined to stick it out'.

On 21 November the squadron changed aerodromes for the last time, flying to Béthencourt. On 3 January 1919, on a practise flight, Edward Graham crashed and was killed. He was the squadron's last casualty in France. Over four days, from 20 January, No 56 Sqn's SE 5as were flown to Le Hameau. Pilots and ground personnel gradually departed. On 2 February the final order came. The squadron was to be reduced to cadre status on the 5th. The day was dismal, snow lay on the ground and there was low cloud. Speaks and Clarkson left with the squadron's remaining transport. Grinnell-Milne, the last to leave, watched the lorries take the long straight road to Cambrai. No 56 Sqn RFC/RAF had ceased to exist as a fighter unit.

Johnny Speaks with his SE 5a H677 '2', which was one of the last SE 5as to be issued to No 56 Sqn

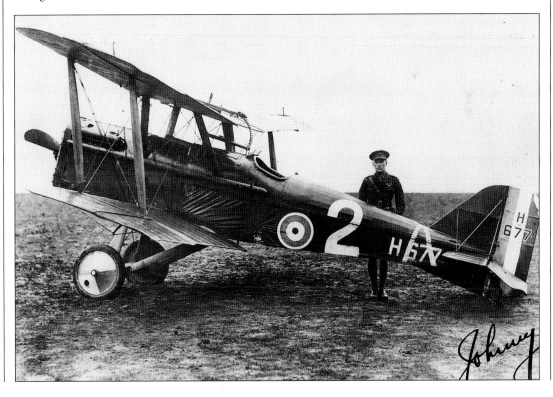

APPENDICES

APPENDIX 1

No 56 SQN COMMANDERS IN FRANCE

Maj Richard Graham Blomfield – 6/2/17 to 29/10/17
Maj Rainsford Balcombe Brown – 29/10/17 to 2/5/18*
Maj Euan James Leslie Warren Gilchrist – 5/5/18 to 17/12/18
Capt Duncan William Grinnell-Milne – 17/12/18 to 5/2/19

* Killed in action

APPENDIX 2

No 56 SQN AERODROMES

Formed Gosport, England, 8/6/16
To London Colney, England, 14/7/16
To Vert Galant, France, 7/4/17
To Liettres (Estrée Blanche), France, 31/5/17
To Bekesbourne, England, 21/6/17
A Flight to Rochford, England, 22/6/17
A Flight to Bekesbourne, England, 4/7/17
To Liettres, France, 5/7/17
To Laviéville, France, 12/11/17
To Baizieux, France, 21/1/18
To Valheureux, France, 25/3/18
To Lechelle, France, 15-16/10/18
To Esnes, France, 27/10/18
To La Targette, France, 29/10/18
To Béthencourt (Beauvois), France, 21/11/18
Cadre to Narborough, England, 5/5/19
Cadre to Bircham Newton, England, 30/12/19
Disbanded Bircham Newton, England, 22/1/20

APPENDIX 3

No 56 SQN's WINGS AND BRIGADES

6th Wing (6th Brigade) – 8/6/16
18th Wing Training Brigade – 14/7/16
9th Wing (GHQ BEF) – 7/4/17
6th Brigade (Horse Guards) – 21/6/17
13th Wing (3rd Brigade BEF) – 12/11/17

APPENDIX 4

No 56 SQN's TOP-SCORING PILOTS

(Note – Victories scored only while serving with No 56 Sqn)

Capt J T B McCudden – 51
Lt R T C Hoidge – 27
Capt G J C Maxwell – 26
Lt A P F Rhys Davids – 25
Capt G H Bowman – 22
Capt R A Maybery – 21
Lt L M Barlow – 20
Capt H J Burden – 16
Capt C M Crowe – 14
Lt M E Mealing – 14
Capt A Ball – 13
Capt W R Irwin – 11
Lt T Durrant – 10
2Lt R H Sloley – 9
Capt E W Broadberry – 8
Lt K W Junor – 8
Lt C A Lewis – 8
2Lt K K Muspratt – 8
Capt L W Jarvis – 7
Lt H J Walkerdine – 7
Capt W S Fielding-Johnson – 6
Capt P B Prothero – 6
Capt W O Boger – 5
Capt D Grinnell-Milne – 5
Lt C H Jeffs – 5
Lt H A S Molyneux – 5

APPENDIX 5

No 56 SQN CASUALTIES

Killed in action – 44

Wounded in action and died of wounds – 3

Wounded in action – 19

Prisoners of war and died of wounds – 1

Prisoners of war and wounded – 8

Prisoners of war – 20

Killed in flying accidents – 3

Injured in flying accidents and died of injuries – 1

Injured in flying accidents – 11

Name	Remarks	Date	Aeroplane Serial
1917			
2Lt M A Kay	Killed	30 April	A4866
2Lt R M Chaworth-Musters	Killed	7 May	A4867
Capt A Ball	Killed	7 May	A4850
Capt H Meintjes	Wounded	7 May	A8900
Lt J O Leach	Wounded	7 May	A4856
2Lt H F W Bailey	Injured	9 May	A4854
Lt A J Jessop	Killed	12 May	A4860
Lt C E French	PoW Wounded	20 May	A8912
2Lt J Toogood	PoW Wounded	26 May	A8902
2Lt E A Lloyd	PoW Wounded	27 May	A8905
2Lt G M Wilkinson	Wounded	28 May	A8899
Lt T M Dickinson	POW Wounded	4 June	A8920
Lt H Hamer	Killed	6 June	A8899
Lt H Rogerson	PoW	14 June	A8919
2Lt K J Knaggs	Wounded	16 June	A8911
2Lt H G Spearpoint	PoW	17 June	A4862
Lt W Turner-Coles	PoW	17 June	A8922
Lt C A Lewis	Wounded	7 July	A4853
2Lt J S Turnbull	Wounded	12 July	A4861
Capt E W Broadberry	Wounded	12 July	A8918
Capt E D Messervy	Killed	20 July	A8945
2Lt R G Jardine	Killed	20 July	A8921
Capt P B Prothero	Killed	26 July	A8925
2Lt T W White	PoW	27 July	A8911
2Lt G Ross-Soden	Wounded	9 August	A4563
2Lt I C MacGregor	Injured	9 August	B512
Capt W A Fleming	Killed	10 August	A8923
2Lt D A Page	Killed	14 August	B'509
Lt J G Young	PoW	14 August	A8943
Lt R T Leighton	PoW Wounded	17 August	B514
Lt D S Wilkinson	PoW Wounded	17 August	A8903 (see Note 1)
Capt H M Rushworth	PoW	18 August	B517
2Lt N H Crow	Killed	14 September	B516
Lt W J Potts	Killed	21 September	B4857

Name	Remarks	Date	Aeroplane Serial
2Lt R H Sloley	Killed	1 October	A8928
Lt C H Jeffs	PoW	5 October	B524
2Lt G M Wilkinson	Killed	10 October	B23
2Lt R J Preston-Cobb	Killed	11 October	B542
Lt J N Cunningham	Wounded	11 October	A4861 (see Note 2)
Lt J D Gilbert	Killed	18 October	B528
Lt G B Shone	Wounded	18 October	B588 (see Note 3)
2Lt A P F Rhys Davids	Killed	27 October	B31
Lt F R C Cobbold	PoW Wounded	8 November	B630
Capt P C Cowan	Killed	8 November	B4883
2Lt J P Waters	Killed (accident)	18 November	B502
2Lt A Dodds	PoW	29 November	B4890
2Lt G A Cawson	Killed	30 November	B4871
Capt R T Townsend	Killed	30 November	B40
Lt B W Harmon	Injured	2 December	B45
2Lt I L Roy	Injured	6 December	B567
2Lt G Walker	Injured	15 December	B63
Capt R A Maybery	Killed	19 December	B506

1918

Name	Remarks	Date	Aeroplane Serial
2Lt R G J Stewart	PoW	3 January	C1753
2Lt B McPherson	Injured	13 January	B668
2Lt E H M Fetch	Wounded	19 January	B66
2Lt L J Williams	PoW	28 January	B610
2Lt C E Morgan	Injured	15 February	C9543
2Lt A L Garrett	Injured	6 March	C1754
2Lt D Woodman	Killed	11 March	B54
2Lt K J Knaggs	Killed	16 March	B121
2Lt W Porter	Killed	24 March	C5389
Lt M E Mealing	Killed	24 March	B182
2Lt W S Maxwell	Killed	27 March	B119
Lt F Beaumont	PoW	1 April	C5433
2Lt B McPherson	PoW	1 April	C6351
2Lt H J Walkerdine	Wounded	11 April	C5432
Capt K W Junor	Killed	23 April	C1086
Maj R Balcombe Brown	Killed	2 May	C1796
Lt B W Harmon	Killed	10 May	D5993
Capt T Durrant	Killed	16 May	B183
2Lt J H Acton	Injured	22 May	C5435
2Lt F C Tarbutt	Killed	16 June	D6088
2Lt H J Mulroy	Killed	18 June	D6098
2Lt A L Garrett	PoW	28 June	B4821
Lt O C Holleran	Wounded	28 June	C5434
2Lt H Austin	PoW Wounded	28 June	D6086
2Lt W Oram	Killed (accident)	8 July	C9583
Capt L N Franklin	Killed	14 July	D6064
Lt T J Herbert USAS	Wounded	8 August	B8423
2Lt H Allen	Killed	10 August	E1286
Capt W O Boger	Killed	10 August	B8429

Name	Remarks	Date	Aeroplane Serial
Lt H T Flintoft	PoW	10 August	D6094
Lt J J Offutt USAS	Killed (accident)	13 August	B179
2Lt V H Hervey	Wounded	13 August	?
Lt T D Hazen	Killed	19 August	E1348
Lt R H Ellis USAS	PoW	21 August	C8884
2Lt N F Bishop	Wounded	21 August	D6126
Lt H J W Roberts	PoW	24 August	B8414
2Lt D C Collier	Killed	24 August	D6121
Lt W M Strathearn	PoW	2 September	C8706
2Lt A Vickers	Killed	3 September	E4064
Capt W R Irwin	Wounded	15 September	D338
Lt L G Bowen	Killed	15 September	C8866
Capt O C Holleran	PoW	15 September	E1291
2Lt N F Bishop	Killed	16 September	B8499
Lt S H Joelson	Injured	20 September	E4063
2Lt J C Gunn	PoW	22 September	C8864
Lt F A Sedore	Wounded	24 September	F5488
Lt G O Mackenzie	Killed	27 September	F5495
Lt J C Speaks	Wounded	28 September	F854
Lt J A Pouchet	Killed	5 October	E5708
Lt I W Awde	PoW Wounded	5 October	H7253
Lt M H Winkler	PoW	21 October	F5463
Lt A S Middleton	Died of Injuries	25 October	E4081
2Lt T H Rogers	Killed	27 October	C6464
2Lt O Price	Killed	4 November	F6276
Lt R F Shutes	Wounded	4 November	F5631
2Lt J C Crawford	Wounded	9 November	E5795 (See Note 4)
2Lt R R Macdonald	Injured	13 November	H7261

1919

| Lt E W Graham | Killed (accident) | 3 January | E5900 |

Notes

1 – Lt D S Wilkinson died of wounds on 26 August 1917 while a PoW

2 – Lt J N Cunningham died of wounds on 18 October 1917

3 – Lt G B Shone died of shock due to severe burns on 19 October 1917. His machine came down in flames after a combat with enemy aeroplanes

4 – 2Lt J C Crawford died of wounds on 12 November 1918

APPENDIX 6

No 56 SQN CASUALTIES – AN EVALUATION OF GERMAN VICTORY CLAIMS

Date	Casualty	Victor
1917		
30 April	M A Kay	Ltn Mallinckrodt *Jasta* 20 (Mallinckrodt badly wounded in the action)
7 May	H Meintjes	No conclusion
7 May	R M Chaworth-Musters	Ltn Werner Voss *Jasta* 'Boelcke'
7 May	A Ball	Accident, pilot error
7 May	J O Leach (wounded)	Ltn Karl Allmenroder *Jasta* 11
12 May	A J Jessop	*KFlakbattr* 101U *Flakzug* 159
20 May	C E French	*Flakbattr* 527 Hptm Holzer
26 May	J Toogood	Vfw Deiss and Uffz Woidt *Schusta* 19
27 May	E A Lloyd	Ltn Altmaier *Jasta* 33
4 June	T M Dickinson	Vfw Wittekind *Jasta* 28
6 June	H Hamer	Vfw Franke *Jasta* 8
14 June	H Rogerson	Ltn Kuppers *Jasta* 6
17 June	H G Spearpoint	Vfw Krebs *Jasta* 6
17 June	W Turner-Coles	Uffz Heidingsfelder and Ltn Romberg *Fl Abt (A)* 292
12 July	E W Broadberry	Wounded in action by elements of *Jasta* 6
12 July	J S Turnbull	Wounded in action by elements of *Jasta* 6
20 July	R G Jardine	ObFmt Schonfelder *Jasta* 7 or Ltn Kroll *Jasta* 24
20 July	E D Messervy	ObFmt Schonfelder *Jasta* 7 or Ltn Kroll *Jasta* 24
26 July	P B Prothero	Vfw Muth *Jasta* 27
27 July	T W White	Ltn Zeigler *Jasta* 26
10 August	W A Fleming	Ltn Stock *Jasta* 6
14 August	J G Young	Ltn Adam *Jasta* 6
14 August	D A Page	Oblt Dostler *Jasta* 6
17 August	D S Wilkinson	Offz Stv Müller *Jasta* 28
17 August	R T Leighton	Ltn Gross *Jasta* 11
18 August	H M Rushworth	Gefr Müller and Uffz Elschenbroich *Schusta* 11
14 September	N H Crow	Ltn Julius Schmidt or Vfw Karl Menckhoff of *Jasta* 3
21 September	W J Potts	Ltns Hack and Klostermann Fl Abt (A) 277
1 October	R H Sloley	Ltn Danhuber *Jasta* 26
5 October	C H Jeffs	Oblt Bruno Loerzer *Jasta* 26
10 October	G M Wilkinson	Ltn Danhuber *Jasta* 26
11 October	R J Preston-Cobb	Ltn Hoyer *Jasta* 36
18 October	J D Gilbert	Ltn Udet *Jasta* 37
18 October	G B Shone	Vfw Kampe *Jasta* 27
27 October	A P F Rhys Davids	Ltn Gallwitz *Jasta* 'Boelcke'
8 November	F R C Cobbold	Ltn Fritz Loerzer *Jasta* 26
8 November	P C Cowan	Ltn von Habler *Jasta* 36
29 November	A Dodds	Ltn Schubert *Jasta* 6
30 November	G A Cawson	Vfws Voigt and Kruse *Schusta* 12
30 November	R T Townsend	Vfw Josef Mai *Jasta* 5
19 December	R A Maybery	*Kflakbattr* 108 Ltn Thiel
1918		
3 January	R J G Stewart	Ltn Hanstein *Jasta* 35

Date	Casualty	Victor
28 January	L J Williams	Ltns Schuppau and Schandva *Abt (A)* 233
11 March	D Woodman	Vfw Scholz *Jasta* 11
16 March	K J Knaggs	Vfw Steinemeyer and Ltn Tittmann *Fl Abt (A)* 240
24 March	W Porter	Ltn Schmid *Jasta* 34 or Oblt Greim *Jasta* 34
24 March	W E Mealing	No conclusion
27 March	W S Maxwel	Ltn Vallendor *Jasta* 'Boelcke'
1 April	F Beaumont	Vfw Könnecke *Jasta* 5
1 April	B McPherson	Hptm Reinhard *Jasta* 6
23 April	K W Junor	Ltn Koepsh *Jasta* 4
2 May	R Balcombe Brown	Ltn Loewenhardt *Jasta* 10
10 May	B W Harmon	Vfw Rumey *Jasta* 5
16 May	T Durrant	Ltn d R Kirschstein *Jasta* 6
16 June	F C Tarbutt	Possibly structural failure
18 June	H J Mulroy	*KFlakbattr* of German 17th Army
28 June	A L Garrett	*KFlakbattr* 7 Vfw Neumann
28 June	H Austin	Ltn d R Thuy *Jasta* 28
14 July	L N Franklin	Ltn Enke and Vfw Leopold, unit unknown
10 August	W O Boger	Possibly Ltn Veltjens or Ltn Borck of *Jasta* 15
10 August	H T Flintoft	Flak, no conclusion
10 August	H Allen	Uffz Lohrmann *Jasta* 42
19 August	T D Hazen	Vfw Mai *Jasta* 5
21 August	R H Ellis	Groundfire
24 August	D C Collier	Vfw Könnecke *Jasta* 5
24 August	H J W Roberts	Groundfire
2 September	V M Strathearn	Vfw Fruhner *Jasta* 26
3 September	A Vickers	Possibly Vfw Hubner *Jasta* 36
15 September	L G Bowen	Groundfire
15 September	O C Holleran	Groundfire
16 September	N F Bishop	Ltn Marcard *Jasta* 26
22 September	J C Gunn	Flak
27 September	G O Mackenzie	Ltn Bassenge *Jasta* 'Boelcke'
5 October	I W Awde	Flak
5 October	J A Pouchet	Flak
21 October	M H Winkler	No conclusion
27 October	T H Rogers	No conclusion. In combat with Fokker D VIIs
4 November	O Price	Oblt Bolle *Jasta* 'Boelcke'
9 November	J C Crawford	Ltn Stark *Jastaführer Jasta* 35b

Glossary of Terms

Fl Abt (Flieger Abteilung) – Aviation unit or Field Flying section for reconnaissance and photography

Fl Abt (A) (Flieger Abteilung Artillery) – Aviation unit cooperating with artillery

Jadgstaffel (Jasta) – Fighter unit

Jagdstaffeln – Fighter units

Jagdgeschwader (JG) – Group of four *Jagdstaffeln* (approximately 50 aeroplanes)

Kraftwagenflak (K-Flak) – Mobile anti-aircraft gun

Luftstreitkräfte – Air Force

Schutzstaffel (Schusta) – Unit of two-seater aeroplanes for the protection of *Flieger Abteilung* and *Flieger Abteilung (A)* aeroplanes

Schlachtstaffel (Schlasta) – *Schutzstaffeln* were renamed *Schlachtstaffel* in March 1918

COLOUR PLATES

1

SE 5 A4850 of Capt Albert Ball, London Colney, England, 6 April 1917

This SE 5 was extensively modified at London Colney through the fitment of a new centre section. Boasting an enlarged trailing edge cutout, it also incorporated an internal gravity-fed petrol tank fitted within the upper wing. Controls to the tailplane were altered and the high seat replaced by one that had the pilot sat lower in the cockpit. 'Bristol type' wheels where introduced and a small head-fairing added behind the cockpit. The Vickers gun and its Constantinesco gear were removed and their position on the top of the fuselage faired over. An extra Lewis gun was installed to fire downwards through the floor of the cockpit. The large windscreen was also discarded, being replaced with a smaller one of the 'Avro' type. None of these modifications was approved by Wing, however, and A4850 was returned to near standard configuration on 9 April 1917. Albert Ball was killed in A4850 on 7 May 1917.

2

SE 5 A4862 of Capt Reginald T C Hoidge, London Colney, England, 6 April 1917

This SE 5 is depicted here in the original standard form as it was received from the Royal Aircraft Factory by No 56 Sqn at London Colney in March 1917.

3

SE 5 A4855 of 2Lt Clarence R W Knight, London Colney, England, 7 April 1917

2Lt Clarence Knight flew this SE 5 to France on 7 April 1917. It was badly damaged during a rough landing on 4 May 1917 and returned to No 2 Aeroplane Supply Depot (ASD).

4

SE 5 A4563 of 2Lt Arthur P F Rhys Davids, Bekesbourne, England, July 1917

This was the prototype SE 5a powered by a 200 hp Hispano-Suiza engine. Shown here in the markings of Rhys Davids, the scout was later flown by Verschoyle Cronyn on the evening of 23 September, when it was badly damaged in the fight with Werner Voss. The aircraft was duly transferred to No 1 ASD following this episode.

5

SE 5 A8913 of Lt K K Muspratt, Bekesbourne, England, July 1917

This SE 5 was flown by Keith Knox Muspratt from 23 May 1917 until it was returned to No 1 ASD on 7 August 1917 for replacement by an SE 5a.

6

SE 5 A8911 of Capt E L L Turnbull, Vert Galant, France, April 1917

A8911 was issued to No 56 Sqn on 7 June 1917 and was struck off strength less than two months later on 27 July 1917 when its pilot, T W White, was shot down and captured. It is shown here in the markings used by E L L Turnbull.

7

SE 5a B4863 of Capt J T B McCudden, Estrée Blanche, France, Autumn 1917

McCudden scored ten victories flying this SE 5a, using it exclusively from 6 September 1917 until he went on leave on 23 October 1917. While McCudden was on leave, A4863 was wrecked by Harry Slingsby when he flew it into a house on 2 November 1917 while landing at night.

8

SE 5 serial unknown, Estrée Blanche, France, August 1917

This SE 5a, serial unknown, was marked with a small red dumbbell on its rear fuselage – the first unit marking issued to No 56 Sqn on 26 August 1917. At this time the flights marked the dumbbells in their colours, with A Flight in white, B Flight in Blue and C Flight in red.

9

SE 5 A8918 of Capt Edric W Broadberry, Estrée Blanche, France, July 1917

This distinctively marked SE 5 was flown by Capt Broadberry, who was at its controls when he was shot down on 14 July 1917. Such markings were rarely seen on SE 5/5as in France, A8918 being one of a number of No 56 Sqn scouts decorated on 10 July 1917 when the unit was grounded due to bad weather. The pilots decided to pass the time by painting their SE 5s in a variety of colour schemes in emulation of the German pilots that they had been meeting over the front. Broadberry's engine mechanic, Len Baker, painted a fearsome dragon (or was it a crocodile!?) on the nose and fuselage of his SE 5, while another machine carried a painting of a Spanish dancer and the name *Conchita*. A third SE 5 was 'striped red and white, and looked like a zebra'. Maxwell's scout had a bright red nose. However, the 9th Wing soon learnt of this 'frivolity' and ordered the schemes to be immediately removed.

10

SE 5a B502 of Capt Gerald J C Maxwell, Estrée Blanche, France, Summer 1917

This SE 5a was initially flown by Gerald Constable Maxwell, who scored ten of his 26 victories while flying it. On 18 November 1917, B502 was crashed by John Waters, who was killed.

11

SE 5a B514 of Lt Richard T Leighton, Estrée Blanche, France, August 1917

This SE 5a was issued to the squadron on 10 August 1917 and was lost just seven days later when Richard Leighton was shot down and captured. The band, in Leighton's family colours, was positioned, coincidentally, in the exact location of the later squadron marking of an 18-inch wide white band, issued on 25 September 1917.

12

SE 5a B4890 of 2Lt Alexander Dodds, Boistrancourt, France, November 1917

This SE 5a was issued to the squadron on 17 November 1917, and it was being flown by Alexander Dodds when he was shot down and captured on 29 November 1917.

13

SE 5a B525 of Capt William S Fielding-Johnson, Estrée Blanche, France, November 1917

This SE 5a was issued to the squadron on 23 August 1917, and it was finally sent to No 2 ASD on 2 February 1918 following months of combat flying, having been declared unfit for frontline service due to its age.

14

SE 5a B630 of Lt Felix R C Cobbold, Estrée Blanche, France, November 1917

Sent to No 56 Sqn on 28 October 1917, this SE 5a was lost on 8 November 1917 when Felix Cobbold was shot down and taken prisoner.

15

SE 5a B4880 of Capt Richard A Maybery, Laviéville, France, December 1917

Issued to the squadron on 11 December 1917, this SE 5a was assigned to A Flight Commander Richard Maybery. He had personally collected this machine from No 2 Aeroplane Supply Depot and had it marked with the flight commander's letter. At 1215 hrs on 19 December the scout's engine was 'not running very well', so Maybery hastily switched to SE 5a B506 and led his flight off on patrol. Having claimed his 21st victory early on in the mission, Maybery was killed by flak a short while later.

16

SE 5a B4891 of Capt J T B McCudden, Baizieux, France, March 1918

B4891 was assigned to No 56 Sqn on 3 December 1917 and flown by James McCudden, who fine-tuned the engine and fitted a red spinner taken from an LVG that he had downed on 30 November 1917 – one of no fewer than 32 victories that McCudden scored in this machine. The flight letter 'G' was replace by the numeral '6' when B Flight changed its markings on 29 December 1917.

17

SE 5a C5303 of Lt Leslie N Franklin, Baizieux, France, March 1918

This SE 5a, issued to No 56 Sqn on 9 November 1917, was flown by Leslie Franklin until it was written off in a crash on 16 March 1918.

18

SE 5a B595 of Capt Maurice E Mealing, Baizieux, France, March 1918

B595 was issued to the squadron on 11 October 1917. It survived the autumn and winter, and was eventually struck off strength on 16 March 1918 after a spar was broken while diving in pursuit of an enemy machine.

19

SE 5a B628 of Capt William R Irwin, Baizieux, France, March 1918

This SE 5a was issued to the squadron on 11 February 1918. It was crashed on landing by William Irwin on 18 March 1918 and struck off strength.

20

SE 5a C5430 of Capt Louis W Jarvis, Valheureux, France, April 1918

This SE 5a was issued to the squadron on 13 March 1918 and flown by Louis Jarvis until 12 April, when it crashed due to engine failure and was returned to No 2 ASD.

21

SE 5a C6351 of 2Lt Barclay McPherson, Valheureux, France, April 1918

Issued to the squadron on 12 March 1918, C6351 was lost on 1 April 1918 when its pilot, Barclay McPherson, was shot down and made a PoW.

22

SE 5a B183 of Capt Trevor Durrant, Valheureux, France, May 1918

Trevor Durrant flew this SE 5a from 25 March 1918 until his death on 16 May 1918, claiming eight of his eleven victories in B183.

23

SE 5a B144 of Capt Cyril Parry, Valheureux, France, June 1918

Cyril Parry flew this SE 5a from 24 February 1918 until it was damaged in combat on 7 June 1918 and returned to No 2 ASD.

24

SE5a C1096 of Capt Henry J Burden, Valheureux, France, August 1918

This SE 5a was delivered to No 56 Sqn on 28 March 1918 and assigned to Henry Burden. He duly used it to score 13 of his 16 victories. C1096 was struck off strength on 21 August 1918.

25

SE 5a C8866 of Lt Laurence G Bowen, Valheureux, France, September 1918

This SE 5a was issued to the squadron on 20 August 1918 and flown by Larry Bowen until 15 September, when he was killed in action.

26

SE 5a H677 of Capt John C Speaks, Bethencourt, France, October 1918

H677 was flown by John Speaks from 30 October 1918 until 20 January 1919, when it was despatched to Le Hameau for disposal.

27

SE 5a E5808 of Lt William E Clarkson, Le Hameau, France, January 1919

This SE 5a was issued to the squadron on 25 October 1918 and flown to Le Hameau for disposal by William Clarkson on 20 January 1919.

28

SE 5a C1149 of Capt Duncan W Grinnell-Milne, Le Hameau, France, January 1919

C1149 was delivered to No 56 Sqn on 21 October 1918 and flown by Grinnell-Milne, who had an unpainted spinner fitted and *SCHWEINHUND* painted in white on the nose. The propeller boss was painted red with thin white borders. Following the Armistice, Grinnell-Milne had C1149's entire fuselage and tailplane painted red. He eventually flew this machine to Le Hameau for disposal on 23 January 1919.